FLAMES and EXPLOSIONS

An Introduction to Teaching Chemistry from Demonstration-Experiments

featuring

The Fundamental Antithesis of Science
between
Evidence and Inductions

and

THE BIG THREE
Flammable Gases
Liquid Nitrogen
and Dry Ice

plus

The Kinetic-Molecular Model of Matter

The Last Lectures
of
Henry A. and Henry E. Bent

Henry A. Bent

Order this book online at www.trafford.com
or email orders@trafford.com

Most Trafford titles are also available at major online book retailers.

Printed in the United States of America.

ISBN: 978-1-4907-4181-9 (sc)
ISBN: 978-1-4907-4182-6 (e)

Library of Congress Control Number: 2014912484

Trafford rev. 07/15/2014

 www.trafford.com

North America & international
toll-free: 1 888 232 4444 (USA & Canada)
fax: 812 355 4082

Other Books by Bent

The Second Law: An Introduction to Classical and Statistical Thermodynamics, Oxford University Press, 1965

New Ideas in Chemistry from Fresh Energy for the Periodic Law, AuthorHouse, 2006

MOLECULES and the Chemical Bond (Volume I), Trafford Publishing, 2011

MOLECULES and the Chemical Bond: An Introduction Conceptual Valence Bond Theory, Volume II, Third Edition, Trafford Publishing, 2014.

PREFACE

This book is transcriptions of the last lectures of Henry A. and Henry E. Bent, on flames and explosions, and -

The Triangle of Chemical Education

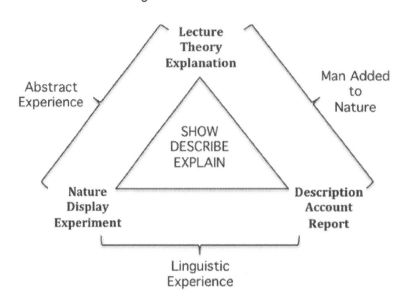

Education in chemistry occurs best when the three components of the "Triangle"—an experiment, a description of the experiment, and an explanation of the experiment—*are at the same place at the same time*. Lectures in a main chemistry building on Mondays, Wednesdays, and Fridays and labs in another building on Tuesdays or Thursdays are not the same experience.

Stressed is Whewell's fundamental antithesis of science between things and thoughts, evidence and inductions, illustrated by demonstration-experiments that feature -

THE BIG THREE

Flammable Gases
Liquid Nitrogen
Dry Ice
and
The Kinetic-Molecular Model of Matter

The enthusiasm of student-apprentice-presenters for executing the "Triangle" ("The best thing that happened to me in school this past year") and the enthusiasm for those presentations of audiences of all ages and socioeconomic backgrounds—especially street-wise inner-city youths who like to do things and see what happens—suggests elevating education in chemistry and, simultaneously, sparking interest in science in sparkable youths by means of *well-mentored student-teams motivated to learn chemistry in order to execute safely and to explain correctly in terms of the kinetic-molecular model of matter striking demonstration-experiments for peers, younger students, and the general public.* It's a winner for all lives it touches: "exactly what our students need," said a middle school teacher, "and we can't give them."

A SHORT TABLE OF CONTENTS

Preface

Contents
FLAMES AND EXPLOSIONS
Part 1
Excerpts from Henry A. Bent's Faraday Lectures
Pittsburgh 1990-1992, 2000

FLAMES AND EXPLOSIONS
Part 2
Henry E. Bent's Last Lecture in Chemistry 1
University of Missouri – Columbia, 1971

Concluding Comments

One virtue of teaching general chemistry from demonstration-experiments in the manner cited above is an absence of a leading source of perplexity among chemistry students: namely, *atomic orbitals*, necessarily accepted on faith, in most instances. Introductory chemistry courses based on uses of atomic orbitals are, accordingly, for most newcomers to the subject, faith-based courses.

FLAMES AND EXPLOSIONS
Part 1

Student: "Are you going to talk about atoms and molecules?"
Presenter: "That's all we are going to talk about."

Content, Occasions, Location, Audiences, and Sponsors: Selections from Faraday Christmas Lectures by Henry A. Bent in Pittsburgh's Soldiers and Sailors Memorial Auditorium for Honor Students in Chemistry from Western Pennsylvania, Eastern Ohio, and Northern West Virginia, supported by the Society of Analytical Chemists of Pittsburgh, the Spectroscopy Society of Pittsburgh, and the Department of Chemistry, University of Pittsburgh.

Purpose. To spark interest in science in sparkable youths by safe execution of striking demonstration-experiments and their explanations in terms of kinetic-molecular theory.

Setting. A large stage beneath a high ceiling fronted by a colorful display of floating balloons, with half a dozen large rectangular tables supporting and surrounded by an array of demonstration equipment including: large tanks of gases (hydrogen, helium, oxygen, nitrogen, methane, and propane) chained to dollies, large fire extinguishers, fire blankets, explosion shields, protective metal shields for table tops, spare goggles, face masks, ear muffs, propane torches, bottle-rocket launching rods, cannons, large tall glass flasks, hot plates with magnetic stirrers, plastic buckets, a large Dewar of liquid nitrogen, a large chest of dry ice, a large fish bowl of rectangular cross section, a large bell jar, a Plexiglas-sided candle stair case, molecular models, posters, an overhead projector, bottles and cans of chemicals, &c. Also familiar things (used in unfamiliar ways), including: balloons, candles, tennis balls, pop bottles, kitchen pan, kitchen towel, air, and water. Briefly put, THE BIG THREE: Flammable Gases, Liquid Nitrogen, and Dry Ice and equipment to exhibit their behavior.

Hands-On/Eyes-On Anticipatory Events for an Arriving Audience: A Preview of Coming Attractions: Crushing by hand of liquid-nitrogen-cooled flowers; watching balloons containing or attached to flasks containing subliming dry ice expand (and burst); ignition of soap bubbles filled with hydrogen and hydrogen-oxygen mixtures; ignition of hand-held propane-filled soap bubbles; and a slide show of highlights of the life of Michael Faraday.

Dress Rehearsals. Attended by middle school students and their teachers and, one evening, the general public. The same demos work for all audiences. Chemistry is chemistry. Combustion of hydrogen is the same for middle schoolers as for senior scientists. One merely says different things about it, depending on the sophistication of an audience.

Presenters. Staff of a Department of Chemistry's Outreach Program. Usually included: the program's director, a post-doctoral fellow, a visiting professor, a high school teacher on sabbatical leave, several graduate and undergraduate students, and, to handle lights and recording equipment, several volunteers from SACP and SSP.

Boxed statements stand for posters or projected images, on a large screen.

Text statements in **bold face** are descriptions of demonstration-experiments.
Statements in small type are messages for the reader.

P1 Principal Presenter 1
P2 Principal Presenter 2

Host (Current chairman of the SACP/SSP Faraday Lecture Committee). Signals end of Anticipatory Events. Tells youths standing in line (usually a long line) that ignitions of soap-bubbles filled with flammable gases will resume for interested individuals at the end of the main program. Thanks providers of equipment. Introduces **P1** and **P2**, briefly!

P1 Welcome to Faraday Lecture 2000. It follows in the footsteps of Michael Faraday and his famous Christmas Lectures for Juvenile audiences at the Royal Institution about, in his words, *The Chemical History of the Candle.*

The star of our program is in this tank.

P1 places an arm around a tank of hydrogen.

We can learn a lot about it just by observing the character of its container.
It has only curved surfaces, top and sides, and bottom, also,
concave inward, so that the tank can be stood upright, if somewhat precariously, hence this chain.

P2 unchains the tank from its dolly and, with P1's help, exhibits its bottom.

P2 The tank is pretty heavy. One might guess that it has thick walls.

P1 Access to the tank's contents is by means of a valve, at its top, protected by this sturdy screw cap.

P1 unscrews the cap, revealing a valve, to which he attaches reducing valves,
"to reduce the pressure in steps," and adds that -

> Everything about the tank
>
>   curved surfaces
>   large mass
>   protected valve
>   dolly for moving it about
>   chain to its dolly
>
> suggests the same thing.

P1 *The tank is designed to contain a gas at high pressure* and, *thus, many molecules.* For, as you know, -

> For ideal gases
>
> $$PV = nRT$$
> $$==>$$
> $$n = P(V/RT).$$
>
> Thus, for given V and T,
> if P is large, then n,
> population of molecules,
> is large.

For gases, molecular population is proportional to pressure.

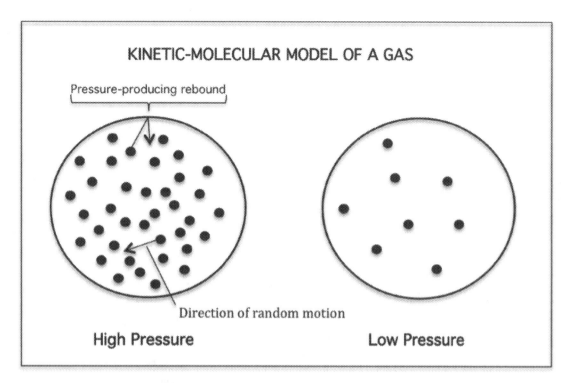

P1 So much we infer from the tank's shape and mass.
   As Yogi Berra has said, "You can observe a lot just by watching."
   The tank's gas is hydrogen.

P2 Evidently hydrogen molecules are not be very sticky toward each other.

P1 In fact, at any temperature merely 23 Celsius degrees, or more, above absolute zero hydrogen cannot be liquefied however high the pressure may be.

P2 The tank is *chained* to its dolly, as we noted, to lessen the chance that it might tip over.

P1 **For, should that happen,** the tank might snap off its valve if it struck something on the way down.

P2 Created would be a rocket.

P1 It's happened. One time a tank of hydrogen in a chemistry building fell over, snapped off its valve, took off down a long hall, and exited the building through a wall at the far end.

P2 Somewhat like this:

P2 **inflates and releases a balloon.**

P2 As air in the balloon exited one way, the balloon — by Newton's Law of Action and Reaction — moved in the opposite direction.

P1 It's an example of a general rule: Gases tend to expand from regions where their pressure is high (e.g., inside the balloon, somewhat) into regions where the gas pressure is lower (in an auditorium's space outside the balloon).

P2 Here's another example.

P2 inflates a balloon from the tank of hydrogen. Young children are fascinated by that event. They know that balloons don't self-inflate. Yet the person standing near it wasn't blowing into it.

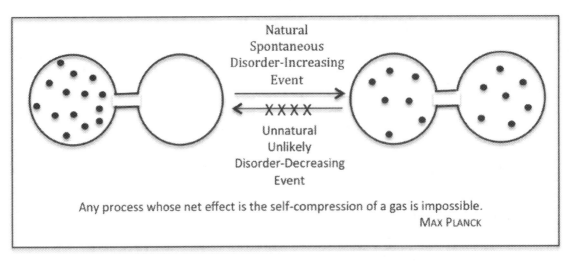

Any process whose net effect is the self-compression of a gas is impossible.
MAX PLANCK

P1 Hydrogen's principal physical property is that it has the lowest density of any known substance, suggested by the fact that a hydrogen-filled balloon *floats in air.*

P2 ties a string to the hydrogen-filled balloon and releases it, holding on to the string.

P1 Here's how we might picture in our minds' eyes what we just saw with our optical eyes.

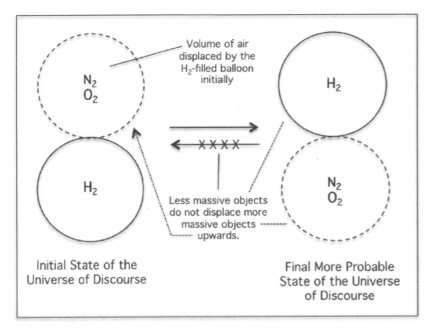

P2 Floating is a matter of density.

P2 has a young volunteer pick up a lead brick and hand it to the presenter.

This heavy brick floats in mercury but not, unlike our hydrogen-filled balloon, in air. Floating in mercury would be easy to show — but safe removal afterwards of small droplets of toxic mercury adhering to the brick, not so much so.

4

P2 drops the lead brick onto an orange crate resting on the auditorium's floor off the front of the stage, smashing it to bits.

P1 As the brick fell, it displaced air upwards, from where the brick ended up to where the brick started its descent.

P1 How is a fallen lead brick like the levitated balloon?
Both events increased the disorder in the universe. (One can always say that.)
The floor and the brick are a bit warmer — and, accordingly, internally, atomically more disordered — after the heat-producing arrested fall than before it.

CARTOON OF THE "LEAD BALLOON" DEMO

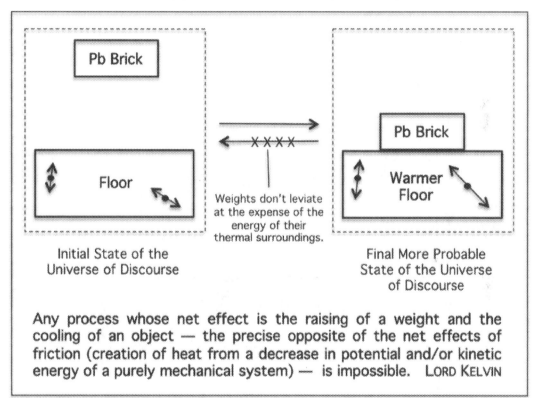

Initial State of the
Universe of Discourse

Weights don't leviate at the expense of the energy of their thermal surroundings.

Final More Probable
State of the Universe
of Discourse

Any process whose net effect is the raising of a weight and the cooling of an object — the precise opposite of the net effects of friction (creation of heat from a decrease in potential and/or kinetic energy of a purely mechanical system) — is impossible. LORD KELVIN

P2 Kelvin's statement generalized applies to all events.

NATURE'S SECOND-LAW-LIKE NATURE

We can't go back.
Time marches onward.
Nature's way is one way.
Nature makes no U-turns.
Movies shown backward look odd.
The Universe never passes through the same state twice.
Any process whose net effects are the opposite of any natural event is impossible.

The entropy of the Universe tends to increase.

P1 Entropy is a numerical measure of atomic and molecular disorder.

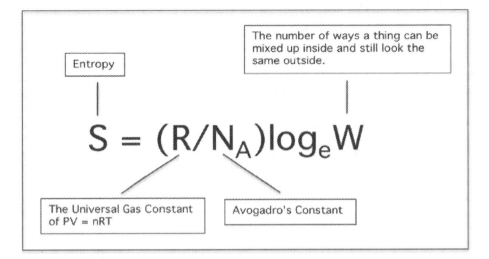

P2 For all natural events -

$$\Delta S_{Universe} > 0$$

P1 An event's entropy-production is a measure of its impact on the environment.

P2 Hence -

> **THE ENTROPY ETHIC**
>
> *Live leanly.*
> *Do not create entropy unnecessarily.*
> *Conserve transformable forms of energy.*

P1 The "Entropy Ethic" addresses most issues regarding man(un)kind's impact on the environment.

P2 Our nation needs a national energy policy.
Our globe needs a personal Entropy Ethic.

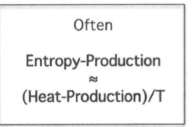

P1 Accordingly, -

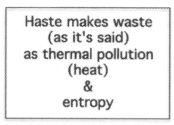

Haste makes waste
(as it's said)
as thermal pollution
(heat)
&
entropy

P2 Walk or ride a bicycle if you can.

Eschew powerful devices, such as 300 horse power internal combustion engines mounted on mobile chasses.

Remember -

Power
=
Rate of change
of
Transformable Energy
to
heat, usually.

P1 Here's the sort of thing that happens inside internal combustion engines.

P1 **torches the hydrogen-filled balloon with a propane torch taped to a pole.**

Balloons and soap bubbles (recommended by Mendeleev) are ideal reaction vessels for explosive reactions whose reactants are gases.

P1 We just saw is a sure fire-demo. Nature is Lawful. Nature always does her thing.

We haven't dominion over Nature.
All we have are opportunities
to work with Nature.

P2 Illustrated by the falling lead brick and combustion of hydrogen is the difference between a physical change and a chemical change.

The atomic rearrangement in the combustion has so profound an effect on participating matter's properties we change the substances' names. We say that -

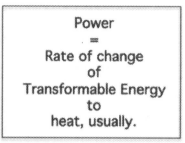

"Hydrogen" + "Oxygen" = "Water" + "Heat"

P1 Here's another illustration of the difference between physical and chemical changes.

P1 **drops a box of matches** and says:
"Free and arrested fall. Physics."

P1 **strikes a match,** and says:
"Combustion! Chemistry!

> Chemistry is more striking than physics.
> Physics is no match for chemistry.

Just joking. There's a lot of physics in combustion.

P2 Combustion illustrates in -

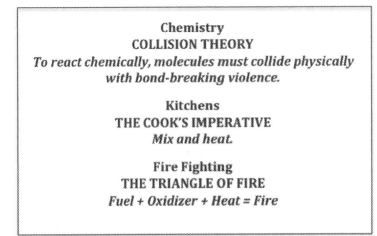

Chemistry
COLLISION THEORY
To react chemically, molecules must collide physically
with bond-breaking violence.

Kitchens
THE COOK'S IMPERATIVE
Mix and heat.

Fire Fighting
THE TRIANGLE OF FIRE
Fuel + Oxidizer + Heat = Fire

P1 For fire, three things must be at the same place at the same time: molecules of fuel, molecules of oxidizer, and activation.

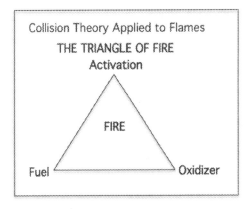

Collision Theory Applied to Flames
THE TRIANGLE OF FIRE
Activation

FIRE

Fuel   Oxidizer

P2 Recall the size of the hydrogen-produced fireball.

P1 It was much larger than the inflated balloon.

P2 The hydrogen had to reach out — or, as we say, diffuse — into the room for its oxygen.

P1 The flame is called, accordingly, a diffusion flame.

P2 The flame of a torch (as usually used) is a pre-mixed flame.

P1 Gaseous propane and air mix down here at these air ports.

P2 **closes the torch's air ports with his hand:** "A bushy, diffusion flame."

P2 **removes his hand from the torch's air ports:** "A hotter, premixed flame."

P1 How about premixing hydrogen and oxygen, in a balloon?

P2 Would it be a safe thing to do?

P1 Hydrogen-oxygen mixtures are said to be explosive.

P2 Yet watch this:

P2 attaches with rubber tubing a hollow glass wand to tank hydrogen's pressure gauge, opens the gauge, slightly, and squirts issuing hydrogen into oxygen-containing air and, for good measure, at the floor, at a sheet of paper, at personal clothing, at his or her hand, face, and hair, and, finally, into a beaker of water.

P1 CONCLUSION: Hydrogen doesn't react with the iron of the steel of its tank,
or with the copper and zinc of its brass pressure gauge,
or with the rubber and glass of this rubber tubing and glass wand,
or with the nitrogen and oxygen of air, or with water.
Nor is it toxic.
(squirts self in the face again).

P2 Briefly put: Hydrogen at *room temperature* is inert stuff.
Faraday was fascinated by the inertness of cold fuels.
"What are they waiting for?" he wondered.

Faraday harbored doubts — some 150 years ago — regarding the reality of atoms and molecules. The kinetic-molecular model of matter and its extraordinary explanatory power was not a functional part of his mental tool kit.

P1 Chemists encode cold hydrogen's inertness with three ideas.

AN EXPLANATION OF COLD HYDROGEN'S INERTNESS

Hydrogen molecules are diatomic.

To react chemically molecules must collide with each other with bond-breaking violence.

The hydrogen-hydrogen bond of dihydrogen is strong.

P2 So, it seems that it would be safe to mix cold hydrogen gas with cold oxygen gas.
For complete reaction, the equation, -

$$2\,H_2 \;+\; O_2 \;=\; 2\,H_2O$$

calls for a molecular ratio of 2-to-1. According to -

AVOGADRO'S LAW

Equal volumes of gas at the same T and P contain equal numbers of molecules.

Accordingly, a 2-to-1 molecular ratio corresponds to a volume ratio of 2-to-1.

Avogadro's Law reflects the fact that from a physical point of view gases are very much alike: *mostly empty space.*

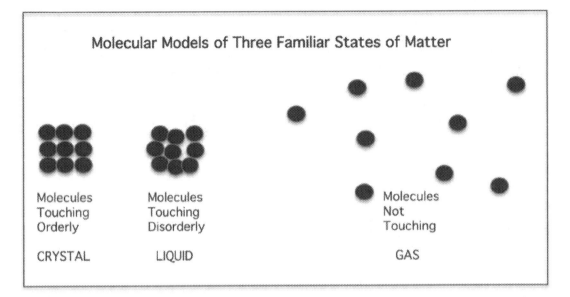

P1 For most gases the ideal gas equation of state, mentioned earlier, is approximately true.

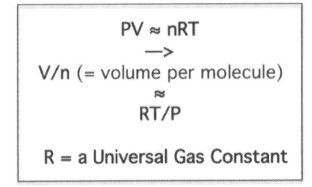

If T and P are the same, then V/n is the same.

P2 We can eyeball the 2-to-1 ratio because, for our purposes, the precise ratio is not important.

Hydrogen, because of its small molecular mass, has the highest random molecular velocities of any gas, the highest flame velocities, and, accordingly, the widest limits of flammability.

P1 Reads from a Handbook of Chemistry and Physics:

Chemical Formula	Limits of Flammability	
	Lower	Upper
H_2	4%	74%

P2 adds oxygen and hydrogen to a balloon, and pauses.

P1 Safety first.

P2 Prudent practice in the laboratory is *imagining,* using one's *memory* of personal *experiences* and memory of additional *knowledge* and by use of *common sense* applied to *observations,* the worst things that might happen, and preparing for them. We call it –

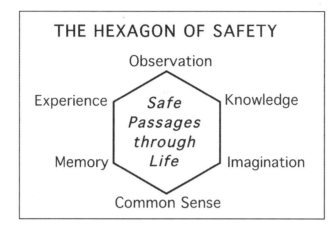

THE HEXAGON OF SAFETY

Observation

Experience

Knowledge

Safe Passages through Life

Memory

Imagination

Common Sense

P1 Do we need rain coats or umbrellas, owing to formation of water?
Not in our experience.
But do cover your ears, to protect ear drums.

P2 dons ear muffs and (finally!) torches the balloon filled with a mixture of hydrogen and oxygen.

BOOM!!

P1 That was <u>explosive</u> formation of water, from hydrogen and oxygen.
Yet no need for raincoats.
It was too hot, in the flame's region, for water molecules to stick together and form droplets of *liquid* water.

Needed in order to show the presence of water molecules,
which are invisible in the gaseous state, as water vapor, or superheated steam,
is a cold, molecule-condensing surface,
for the alleged water molecules to condense on,
such as the glass of this bell jar, at room temperature,
which is cold, compared to water's boiling point,
at which temperature liquid water forms gaseous water, at 1 atm.

P2 sets about filling the bell jar with hydrogen.

P1 We could use a volunteer.

A volunteer places a hand, as requested, up into the bell jar (resting on wooden blocks).

P1 Hot or cold?

"Cold."

P1 At room temperature fast moving hydrogen molecules conduct energy away from warmer bodies, such as a person's hand, faster than do heavier molecules of air;
hence the cool feeling, in hydrogen.

P2 removes a small plug in the end of a short piece of glass tubing that passes
through a rubber stopper that stoppers an opening at the top of the bell jar
and ignites the emerging hydrogen gas.

P1 Hydrogen's flame is nearly colorless.
Hydrogen contains no soot-forming carbon, which, as hot soot, in a candle's flame, glows
(yellow hot).

P2 Now our flame has heated the soft glass tubing and is vaporizing some of its sodium,
which lends a characteristic yellow color to flames.

P1 sprays a sodium chloride solution into the flame of a Fisher burner,
then solutions of chlorides of copper and strontium.

P2 Now *imagine* what's going on with the hydrogen inside our bell jar.
As denser air, attracted gravitationally by the earth, sinks and displaces less dense hydrogen
gas upward and out the exit at the top of the bell jar, air begins to enter the bell jar at its
bottom and mix with hydrogen above it, forming a hydrogen-air mixture, perhaps explosive.

As the hydrogen-air mixture begins to exit the bell jar,
the burning velocity of the flame, no longer a pure diffusion flame, increases.

Eventually the exiting gas's burning velocity exceeds its flow velocity upward,
and the flame advances down the glass tube,
until, cooled by the tube, it retreats upward.
Sometimes rapid up and down oscillations create a high-pitched hum.
As the pitch drops, one senses that the flame is about to make its way all the way down into
the bell jar.

BOOM!!

P1 And what's this?
The bell jar has fogged up!
On the inside or the outside?

A volunteer determines that dew was formed on the bell jar's *interior* surface.

P1 What does the dew feel like?
"Water," volunteers the volunteer.
How much would you estimate that there is?
More than one-hundredth of a milliliter and less than one milliliter?
Say about one-tenth of a milliliter?

P2 0.18 mL of water would be about 0.18 grams of water or one-hundredth of a mole of H_2O,
corresponding, at STP, to 0.224 liters of H_2,
which seems like the right order of magnitude:
more than 0.02 liters and less than 2.2 liters
(as not all the water that was formed condensed on the bell jar's surface).

We see why hydrogen is called "hydro-gen". It's a water-generator.

P1 Has the gas in the bell jar an odor?
Similar to what? A car's exhaust?
Produced by the explosion's high temperature were, evidently, some oxides of nitrogen.

P2 Produced, also, was a displacement to the floor of gloves and towel that had been resting on the table adjacent to the bell jar.

P1 A clever engineer might have a blast with the explosion's blast.

THE ENGINEER'S THEOREM

Any *spontaneous event*,
such as combustion,
can in principle be *harnessed*
to do *useful* work,
such as elevation or acceleration
of ponderable bodies.

P2 jumps up onto a chair.

P1 How was that jump possible?!
Didn't Kelvin say that ponderable bodies don't spontaneously levitate?

P2 But with continued jumping, I'd get "tired". Right? And "hungry".

My jump was possible, thanks to the Engineer's Theorem.

Biochemical reactions amounting, in the end, to oxidation of some of my recent meals,
coupled to upward motion by way of muscle contractions,
tendons' tensions, and bone movements,
provided by Nature through billions of years of evolution,
made possible my jump.

P1 We can harness our "blast" by elevating a ponderable body by using a lighter "bell jar": namely, a drinking fountain's plastic jug that's had its bottom sawed off.

P2 repeats the glass bell jar demo with a plastic "bell jar".

Boom! *Whoosh!*

P2 reaches out casually and catches the descending reaction vessel.

P1 It took off like a rocket.

P2 Let's try a rocket powered with hydrogen mixed with *pure oxygen,* instead of air.

P1 and P2 inflate a balloon with approximately a 2-to-1 mixture of hydrogen and oxygen, squirt it through a tube into an inverted pop bottle, and place the bottle on a launching rod aimed out over the audience.

P1 Aimed upward, the pop bottle rocket can't reach any of you on the ground floor, at high speed. And experience tells us that it won't go as far as the balcony.

P2 activates the pop bottle's contents with a torch, held off to one side by a gloved hand.

P2 In a nutshell, that's pretty much the story of –

> Harnessing the Power of Fire
> by way of steam engines
> (water + heat = voluminous, piston-moving steam)
> to move boats and trains,
> to run pumps to empty mines of water,
> to power looms for fabrication of cloth,
> to run generators of electricity,
> &c.

P1 Here's how to execute the bottle rocket at home.

> Needed for the Bottle Rocket Experiment
>
> - drug-store rubbing alcohol and hydrogen peroxide
> - grocery-store yeast
> - an empty pop bottle and launching rod
> - an ignition source and goggles
> - a warm day — to insure adequate volatilization of your fuel
> - adult supervision

P2 pours about 200 mL of a 3 percent hydrogen peroxide solution into an empty pop bottle; adds yeast; observes fizzing; checks emerging gas with a glowing splint (Pretty!); pours out the "gunk"; pours in a little alcohol; shakes it out (to flush out yeast and the peroxide solution); repeats the alcohol flush, ending with **vigorous downward shaking of the bottle** and the remark:

> *Solids and liquids, as such, don't burn, with a flame.*
> *It's their vapors, mixed with air, that burn.*
>
> Highly nonvolatile carbon, as charcoal, burns,
> but not with production of a flame.

P2 places the charged rocket on its launching pad and, standing off to one side, ignites its charge with a match taped to a yardstick.

Whoosh!

P1 You need, to repeat, warm weather, otherwise you'll have a *fuel-lean mixture*, owing to the low tendency of liquid alcohol to evaporate when it's cold.

P2 Highly volatile ether as rocket fuel yields, at room temperature, a *fuel-rich* mixture. Ether rockets perform best cooled in ice-water prior to launch.

P1 launches an ice-water-cooled ether rocket.

P2 Here's how we decided how much hydrogen peroxide solutionl to use.

A Question from General Chemistry

Estimate the volume of 3% peroxide solution required
for a 1 L alcohol-oxygen rocket.

Assume that, for a good flush, you want 2 liters of oxygen gas.

P1 Our answer is based on atomic weights, chemical formulas, a balanced chemical equation, and the fact that one "mole" of a gas (one "gram formula weight") occupies at standard temperature and pressure 22.4 liters.

Estimate of the Volume of 3 Percent H_2O_2 Required to Supply Oxygen for a 1 Liter Bottle Rocket

$$2 H_2O_2(l) = 2 H_2O(l) + O_2(g)$$

$$2(2\times1 + 2\times16) \text{ g} \qquad 22.4 \text{ L at STP}$$

$$64 \text{ g} \longrightarrow 22.4 \text{ L}$$

$$\approx 6.4 \text{ g} \longleftarrow 2 \text{ L}$$

3 % soln: 3 g H_2O_2 per 100 g soln or 6 g H_2O_2 per 200 g soln

Solution density: ca. 1 g/mL → 200 mL of solution for 2 L O_2

Each volume of 3 % H_2O_2 yields ten times it volume of O_2 gas.

P2 We've burnt two fuels: hydrogen and alcohol.
This tank contains a third fuel: methane, the chief component of natural gas.
It's Nature's simplest hydrocarbon, CH_4, composed of molecules containing one carbon atom and four hydrogen atoms.

P1 **Holds up a valence sphere model of a CH_4 molecule and a conventional ball-and-stick model.**

P2 Here's one route to those models.

Start with a carbon atom, atomic number 6, and four dihydrogen molecules, H_2.
Remove from the carbon atom its four outer electrons.
That yields a carbon atom's small core: C^{+4}.

A Carbon Atom's Electron-Removal Energies (eV)

11.3
24.4
47.9
64.5

392.1 !
490.0 !

Next, remove from each hydrogen molecule one of its protons, H^+.
That yields four hydride ions, H^-

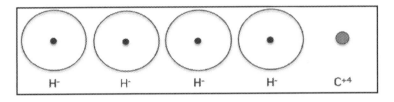

Now ask: What's the best, lowest-energy arrangement for the five charged entities?

Answer: a "tetrahedral arrangement" of the four hydride ions packed as tightly as possible about the carbon core.

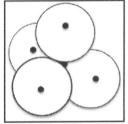

The polarized hydride ions (their protons are slightly off center, owing to repulsion by the carbon core) have become carbon-hydrogen bonds.

P1 Replacing valence spheres by valence strokes and atomic cores (the small black spheres) by symbols of the chemical elements yields a Valence Stroke Representation of the Valence Sphere Model of methane.

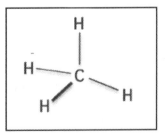

P2 Methane, like hydrogen, is, at room temperature, unreactive toward most substances.

P2 squirts methane at various substances.

P1 Methane is one of a series of hydrocarbons called "paraffins", meaning "lack of affinity".

THE PARAFFINS

C_nH_{2n+2}

For methane, CH_4, n = 1

For hydrogen, H_2, n = 0

n = 3 is propane, 8 octane, followed by oils, greases, paraffin wax, and, for n in the thousands, polyethylene.

P2 Dependence of physical properties upon molecular structure is illustrated, also, by the behavior of sulfur when heated.

P1 At room temperature sulfur is an inert yellow solid, stable in air.
P1 **holds up a chunk of sulfur.**

P1 It's insoluble in water.
P1 **drops a chunk of sulfur into a beaker of water.** It sinks.

P2 Sulfur's molecules, unlike those of its congener oxygen in the Periodic System, are composed of rings of eight atoms.

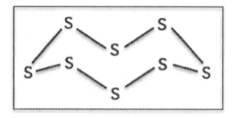

P1 **starts to heat a test tube containing crushed sulfur.**
It melts to a straw-colored liquid.

P2 The liquid is mobile, with a low viscosity.

P1 **sloshes around the liquid in the test tube.**

On continued heating the liquid begins to turn reddish brown.

P2 Sulfur-sulfur bonds are being broken, with formation of light-absorbing centers.

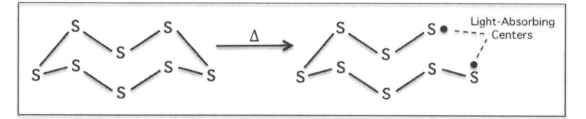

P1 **continues heating.** The liquid continues to deepen in color.

P1 The liquid is becoming viscous.

P2 Chain-like sulfur molecules are beginning to polymerize.

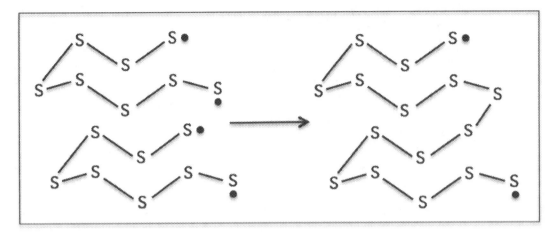

P1 The liquid has become exceedingly viscous.
P1 turns test tube upside down, momentarily, without any liquid running out.

P2 The liquid is highly polymerized.
Its long polymeric molecules are all tangled up with each other.

P1 continues heating the sulfur, which becomes darker and darker in its color as more and more sulfur-sulfur bonds are broken. Eventually, the liquid becomes, again, highly mobile, being now a collection of short sulfur molecules.

P1 I believe it's beginning to boil.

P2 It must be at 444.6 °C (a fixed point on the old centigrade temperature scale).

P1 moves to the front of the stage and, with lights down, pours the test tube's contents, ignited (if necessary) with a flick of the Meeker burner, into a large beaker of water resting on the floor of the auditorium's orchestra pit.

P2 "Fire and brimstone."
In ancient times it was poured onto besiegers storming castles' walls.

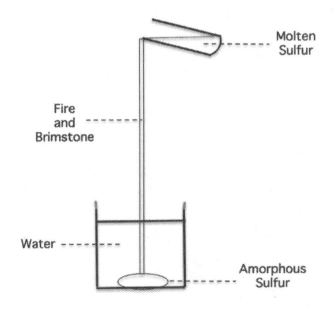

P2 reaches into the beaker, removes some of the amorphous sulfur, and *chews it.* Audience gasps.

P2 It's harmless. It's insoluble in water. It has no flavor.

P2 passes bits of amorphous sulfur to members of the audience.

On being quenched in cold water, the sulfur atoms suddenly repolymerized to a tangled mess of large, flexible molecules. (Sometimes we model sulfur's transformation with audience members holding hands, as divalent sulfur atoms, initially in rings of 8, later as almost single atoms, and, finally, on command, as a tangled mess as they quickly grab, if possible, a nearby hand.)

At room temperature, by breaking and remaking sulfur-sulfur bonds, the sulfur atoms will gradually reconstitute the original octa-atomic S_8 molecules.

Here's how sulfur is mined.

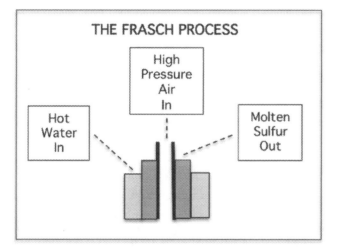

P1 Some gas wells in Canada are as much as 90% hydrogen sulfide, approached carefully! Sulfur is recovered and, in the molten state, run into large enclosures whose walls are raised as the sulfur solidifies, until finally house-size blocks of solid sulfur stand out in the open exposed to rain and snow. Most of it is used in production of sulfuric acid, the world's most widely manufactured chemical.

P2 Back now to our methane and hydrogen.

P1 and P2 bubble their gases into water and adjust rates of bubble-formation until they are nearly the same.

P2 By Avogadro's Law, the gases are emerging from these wands at nearly the same rates: molecule for molecule.

P1 Let's compare their combustibilities.

P1 and P2 flick their wands across a candle's flame.

P2 My methane flame is more luminous than P1's hydrogen flame, owing to soot formation, from the molecules' carbon atoms. Soot is a reaction intermediate, eventually consumed.

My methane flame is, also, the larger of the two flames, because hydrogen molecules require for combustion only one oxygen atom, whereas methane molecules require *four* oxygen atoms.

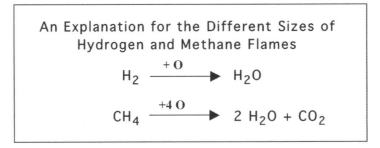

An Explanation for the Different Sizes of Hydrogen and Methane Flames

$$H_2 \xrightarrow{+O} H_2O$$

$$CH_4 \xrightarrow{+4O} 2\,H_2O + CO_2$$

P1 Both flames are, like all diffusion flames, hollow, from the standpoint of combustion.

P1 and P2 hold small squares of wire screens across their flames, aimed at the audience.

P2 blows out the methane flame.

P1 tries but cannot blow out the hydrogen flame.

P2 shakes out the methane flame.

P1 tries but cannot shake out the hydrogen flame.

Every substance is unique, especially hydrogen.

Distinctive Features of Dihydrogen Stemming from Its Low Molecular Weight

- Lightest molecules of any known substance
- Least dense substance
- Least number of electrons per molecule
- Least molar heat capacity of any gas
- Least molar entropy of any gas
- Greatest random molecular speeds (at a given temperature)
- Greatest rate of diffusion
- Greatest thermal conductivity of any gas
- Greatest flame velocities

P2 Blows and shakes are essentially the same experiment.

In a blow, the flame is, in our laboratory's frame of reference, stationary.
The air around it is in motion.

In a shake, the air around the flame is, in our frame of reference, stationary.
The flame is in motion.

P2 turns up methane's flow rate. Its flame front detaches from its wand.

P1 turns up hydrogen's flow rate. Its flame front does not detach from its wand.

P1 shouts (above the hydrogen flame's huge roar):
Hydrogen's mass flow rate never exceeds its flame's burning velocity.

Formed in hydrogen's turbulent flow through air are many small pockets of explosive mixtures of hydrogen and air, hence the noise.

P2 Let's see what happens when a methane-filled balloon is torched.

A volunteer, outfitted with goggles, torches a methane-filled balloon. Audience roars.

Use of volunteers:

        adds variety to programs

        pleases volunteers, peers, and parents

        adds an intriguing air of uncertainty to programs

        increases rapport between presenters and audiences

        suggests that a career in science might be an option for someone interested in science

        illustrates that properly-mentored students could execute the presenters' program, for -

                Nothing done is beyond what young students can do — safely, if well-coached.

                Nothing said is beyond what students can be taught to say.

                Student-presenters may need help, however, with: audiences' questions

                                              Nature's questions

        Even senior scientists are sometimes puzzled when demos don't proceed as expected. Such occasions are excellent teaching moments. Audiences love to see minds in action, attempting to figure out reasons for Nature's behavior, in the belief that there's always a reason for events, in terms of kinetic-molecular theory.

        There aren't "failed experiments", only unimaginative responses to unexpected events.

P1 Raise your hand if you remember feeling heat when the hydrogen-filled balloon was torched. Ditto for the methane-filled balloon.

Hydrogen molecules, recall, contain 2 combustible atoms. Methane molecules contain 5 combustible atoms, one of them carbon.

P2 We can demonstrate carbon's combustibility with a carbohydrate, such as sugar.

P2 pours sugar into a Pyrex test tube to about a depth of an inch;
warms it over the flame of a Meeker burner or a propane torch;
sees the sugar melt to a clear liquid, then caramelize, with
evolution of water that, initially, condenses on upper portions of the test tube.
Finally, the test tube's contents char to a black, refractory solid.

P1 That was another name-changing, "chemical reaction".

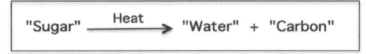

P2 How can we clean this thing out? Carbon is insoluble in ordinary solvents.

A solid substance's ideal solubility in a liquid is lower the higher its melting point.
And carbon has the highest melting point of any known substance.
Carbonized car cylinders used to be cleaned up by *burning* the carbon out.

P2 directs a jet of oxygen through a metal wand toward the test tube's contents, red hot.

P1 I guess one could say: Hot carbon, like hot hydrogen, is combustible, in oxygen!

P2 Well, at least we cleaned out the test tube.
P1 But they won't be happy with it back at the stock room.
P2 Chemistry teachers have christened what we just did "The Bent Test Tube Demo".

P1 Students sometimes ask on such occasions: What's the *largest* flame you can show us?

Unexpected Outcomes of Explosions. In the show-and-tell business for students, bigger is often deemed to be better. Louder is applauded, also. Our loudest explosion? A stoichiometric mixture of methane and oxygen in a balloon collapsed with liquid nitrogen and activated with a propane torch taped to the end of a pole, in a chemistry building's basement storage area. BOOM!!! CRASH!! Oops! There went some shelved glassware in an adjacent storage room. Related in its effect on glassware was detonation in a eudiometer one weekend of an acetylene-oxygen mixture. Owing to the close approach to each other of the carbon C^{+4} cores of triple-bonded acetylene molecules, the molecules are, so to speak, spring loaded. Created, with loud noise, was a harmless powder: the portion of the eudiometer above water level. On another occasion, detonation of a hydrogen-oxygen mixture in an assembly illustrated the power of a shock wave from an explosion, by dislodging an accumulation of soot deposited on a school-building's gymnasium rafters during Pittsburgh's days of steel-making's "hell on earth." For a few moments one couldn't see one's hand before one's face, reported a visitor. "Great Program!" said students, as they left for home to clean up (happily, not difficult to do). "Come again!"

P2 Before exhibiting our largest flame, it might be wise, however, to recall leading facts regarding fire-extinction. Recall the Triangle of Fire.

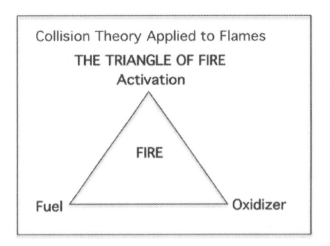

For a fire, all three things must be at the same place at the same time.
Absent fuel, or oxidizer, or activation (usually as heat), absent fire.

P1 Starting at the top: to extinguish a fire, remove the activation.
Cool the fuel and/or the oxidizer.

P2 **blows out a candle's flame.**

P1 To blow out oil well fires, fire fighters use shock waves created by massive charges of high explosives.

P2 Of course, a sure fire way to put out a fire is to *turn off the fuel*.

Sometimes it may be simpler, however, to just let the fire *burn itself out*.

P1 **pours a little diethyl ether onto a volunteer's hand** and asks:
"What's it feel like?"
"Funny."
"Hot or cold?"
"Cold."
"Because evaporation is a heat absorbing event."

P1 **pours diethyl ether on to an empty table top and spreads it about a bit.**

P2 then quickly ignites the ether before its dense vapors pool downward to the audience. After combustion ceases,

P1 **Places his or her hands on the table top,** and reports: "Warm, but not hot."
The diffusion flame never actually touched the table top. Between the two, the flame and the table top, was cold ether vapor, not yet mixed with air and its oxygen.

P2 For most flames oxygen of air is the oxidizer, but not always.

During Britain and Argentina's battle over the Falkland Islands,
a French Exocet missile struck a British cruiser's superstructure,
composed of alloys of light metals, such as magnesium and aluminum,
in order to not overbalance improved and lightened below-deck machinery.
The superstructure caught fire and burned to the deck.
Attempts to smother the fire with water and carbon dioxide,
both of which contain oxygen, for which magnesium and aluminum have huge affinities,
made matters worse.

> **Any substanc that contains oxygen
> is a potential oxidizer,
> especially for substances that have
> huge affinities for oxygen.**

P1 Iron rusts, but not as avidly as freshly exposed magnesium and aluminum do, whose tightly adhering oxide coatings inhibit further oxidation.

P2 **initiates a Thermite Reaction Mixture, composed of powdered iron oxide and aluminum powder,** *behind an explosion shield,* **well away from an audience, with the reaction's molten iron product run into a large beaker of water containing sand at its bottom and a thermometer to register the water's increase in temperature for estimating the difference between heats of formation from elements of consumed ferric oxide and produced aluminum oxide.**

P1 That was iron oxide acting on aluminum and oxidizing it.
The reaction's exothermicity melts the metallic product.

$$2\ Al(s)\ +\ Fe_2O_3(s)\ =\ Al_2O_3(s)\ +\ Heat\ +\ 2\ Fe(l)\ !$$

P1 We've un-rusted iron, so to speak, by roasting its rust in pure aluminum.

P2 Here's another oxygen-atom transfer reaction made famous by a description of an encounter with it as a youth by Ira Remsen. As president of Johns Hopkins University, Remsen introduced to America the PhD research degree, initially in chemistry.

P2 **pours con nitric acid on a copper penny in an Erlenmeyer flask and stoppers it with a water-moistened wad of cotton.**

P1 begins to read Ira Remsen's account of his encounter as a youth with copper and nitric acid.

While reading a textbook of chemistry I came upon the statement, "nitric acid acts upon copper." I was getting tired of reading such absurd stuff and I was determined to see what this meant. Copper was more or less familiar to me, for copper cents were then in use. I had seen a bottle marked nitric acid on a table in the doctor's office where I was then "doing time." I did not know its peculiarities, but the spirit of adventure was upon me. Having nitric acid and copper, I had only to learn what the words "act upon" meant. The statement "nitric acid acts upon copper" would be something more than mere words. All was still. In the interest of knowledge I was even willing to sacrifice one of the few copper cents then in my possession. I put one of them on the table, opened the bottle marked nitric acid, poured some of the liquid on the copper and prepared to make an observation.

P1 continues reading:

But what was this wonderful thing which I beheld? The cent was already changed and it was no small change either. A green-blue liquid foamed and fumed over the cent and over the table. The air in the neighborhood of the performance became colored dark red. A great colored cloud arose.

P2 The dark red-brown gas is nitrogen dioxide. It makes the air over a city of many cars, such as Los Angeles, look brown from approaching, low-flying aircraft.

Nitrogen dioxide is highly water soluble; it is toxic, forming nitric acid in moist lungs; and, at this moment, is being intercepted by the moist cotton "stopper" stuffed in the flask's neck.

P1 reads on:

This was disagreeable and suffocating. How should I stop this? I tried to get rid of the objectionable mess by picking it up and throwing it out of the window. I learned another fact. Nitric acid not only acts upon copper, but it acts upon fingers. The pain led to another unpremeditated experiment. I drew my fingers across my trousers and another fact was discovered. Nitric acid acts upon trousers.

P2 quenches the reaction by adding water to the flask.

"That's purty," said an Ag Campus student.

The "purty" blue color is the aquated copper ion,
present, also, in these crystals of copper sulfate pentahydrate.

Taking everything into consideration, that was the most impressive experiment and relatively probably the most costly experiment I have ever performed. . . . It was a revelation to me. It resulted in a desire on my part to learn more about that remarkable kind of action. Plainly, the only way to learn about it was to see its results, to experiment, to work in a laboratory.

P2 Potassium chlorate, like nitric acid, is powerful, oxygen-rich, oxidizer.
It was one of Mendeleev's favorite reagents in a laboratory.

OXYGEN-RICH REAGENTS AND METALS ACTED UPON

Iron Oxide	Fe_2O_3	Al
Nitric Acid	HNO_3	Cu
Potassium Chlorate	$KClO_3$	Mg

P2 grinds some potassium chlorate with a mortar and pestle, mixes it with magnesium powder, and ignites it in a kitchen pan.

P1 "A flash in a pan." "Flash powder" photographers used to call it.

P1 melts potassium chlorate in a Pyrex test tube behind an explosion shield.

P2 $KClO_3$ has a pyramidal anion. It melts, therefore, at a lower temperature, 356 °C, than does potassium perchlorate, $KClO_4$, whose symmetrical, tetrahedral anion can rotate in the solid state more easily than can the chlorate anion, thereby removing, somewhat, the disorder-creating driving force for melting, which does not occur for $KClO_4$ until 610 °C.

P1 drops into molten $KClO_3$ a piece of hard candy.

P1 That was the chlorate anion oxidizing the carbon and hydrogen of hard candy.

P2 The British Navy's fire-fighters may not have been familiar with -

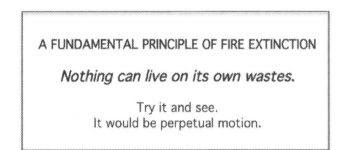

A FUNDAMENTAL PRINCIPLE OF FIRE EXTINCTION

Nothing can live on its own wastes.

Try it and see.
It would be perpetual motion.

P1 Accordingly, fire-fighters usually extinguish fires by smothering them with their usual wastes: oxides of carbon and hydrogen, namely carbon dioxide and dihydrogen oxide.

We can illustrate the Principle with a burner and a beaker.

P1 and P2:

- **Exhibit a Fisher or Meeker burner,** pointing to where gas and air enter the burner.
- **Light the burner, air inlets open.** "A pre-mixed flame."
- **Close air inlets, with a hand.** "A bushy, diffusion flame."
- **Lower a large inverted beaker over the diffusion flame,** soon extinguished.
  "Nothing can live on its own wastes."
- **Lower the beaker over the pre-mixed flame.** It's not extinguished.
  "It's getting its fresh air through its air inlets."
- **Check with a burning splint gases emerging from the beaker inverted over a premixed flame.**
  "The splint's flame is extinguished by the burner's combustion products,
  the same as those of the burning splint."
- **Lower the beaker still further, its rim below the burner's air inlets.**
  The flame goes out. "Again: Nothing can live on its own wastes."
- Remark that the diffusion flame is, from the standpoint of combustion, hollow.
- **Break a small wood match stick in half.**
  Wedge it, coated end upright, into the center of the burner.
  Turn on the gas.
  Wrap a hand about the air inlets.
  Light the emerging gas.
  "The match doesn't catch on fire, in its environment of pure methane."
- **Remove the hand that is blocking the air inlets.**
  The match stick catches fire.
  "Premixed flames are not 'hollow'."
- **Return the hand that was blocking the air inlets.**
  The burning match goes out.
  "Nature has smothered the flame with natural gas."
- **Remove the hand that is blocking the air inlets.** The match catches fire again.

A GENERAL FEATURE OF NATURE'S NATURE
Behavior Depends on Circumstances.

Depending on the circumstances:
  - a person may be happy or sad
  - a match stick may burn or not burn
  - a water molecule may be a proton donor or acceptor
  - an electron may behave like a particle or a wave
  - methane may support combustion or extinguish it

P1 By the way: Nothing in Collision Theory or the Triangle of Fire requires that in a diffusion flame unburnt fuel must be in an inner cone and its oxidizer in the surrounding gas. That arrangement can be reversed.

P2 This apparatus — a large diameter glass tube clamped at an angle with its upper end stoppered with a one-hole stopper — is set up for Nature to produce an "inverted flame".

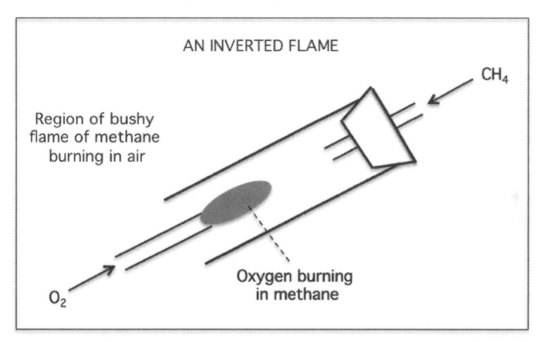

AN INVERTED FLAME

Region of bushy flame of methane burning in air

CH$_4$

Oxygen burning in methane

O$_2$

P1 Directions for using the apparatus:
- Turn on the methane flow.
- Ignite with a torch, *from below*, the methane exiting the apparatus.
- Turn on the oxygen flow.
- Insert the oxygen wand through the flame front of the burning methane.

P2 "Fresh air" for the inverted flame is a combustible gas: say methane.

P1 Before exhibiting our largest flames, let's check the charge of our CO2 fire extinguishers.

P1 and P2 spray nearby audience members with CO2 "snow".

P2 *CAUTION: Be sure the extinguishers are NOT the "dry type"!*

One time a famous lecture-demonstrator inadvertently sprayed an audience with sodium bicarbonate, NaHCO$_3$, a.k.a. baking soda.

P1 Heated (as in a fire) sodium bicarbonate yields, by a proton transfer, sodium carbonate, a.k.a. washing soda, and carbonic acid, which decomposes to water and carbon dioxide.

$$NaHCO_3(s) + NaHCO_3(s) \xrightarrow{\Delta} Na_2CO_3(s) + H_2CO_3$$

H$^+$

$$H_2O + CO_2$$

P1 Supporting that equation are simple kitchen taste tests, before and after heating.

P1 **wets a finger and tastes baking soda on a spatula,** and asks:
Sweet? Bitter? Sour? or salty? Salty, I'd say.

P1 **heats the baking soda on the spatula and, after a moment for cooling, repeats the taste test.**

Sweet? Bitter? Sour? Or Salty? Bitter, I'd say, although it looks to be about the same.
It might be interesting to watch the transformation sometime on the heated stage of a microscope.

P2 Now, back to our CO_2 extinguisher.
Most of the CO_2 inside the extinguisher, if it's freshly charged, is present as a liquid,
under pressure of its own vapor, about 5 atm., at room temperature.

P1 **picks up one of the CO_2 fire extinguishers.**
That pressure of 5 atm is why the surfaces of the CO_2 cylinders are curved,
and it's why, pressurized to only 5 atm, the cylinder's walls are not as thick as those of our
hydrogen cylinder, pressurized to about 100 atm.

Opening a fire extinguisher's valve allows pressurized CO_2 vapor to escape.
Pressure inside the tank decreases.
Liquid CO_2 boils under the reduced pressure of 1 atm.

P2 Boiling is rapid, internal, heat-absorbing, and hence cooling, evaporation, into bubbles of vapor. As the vapor expands, working against the atmosphere, pushing it upward, it cools further. Some of it freezes, to CO_2 snow, at - 78 °C.

P1 Compressed, it's sold as "dry ice":
"ice" because — as some of you may have felt — it's cold;
"*dry*" because — as some of you may have noticed — it doesn't melt, at atmospheric pressure.

P2 Dry ice at atmospheric pressure sublimes. That's how it stays cold. At –78 °C.
That's why we handle it with gloves.

P1 Would it be unsafe to pick up a piece of dry ice, briefly, with a wet hand?
Will it stick, as ice cubes from a refrigerator's freezing compartment do?

P1 **wets a hand, picks up a chunk of dry ice, juggling it.**
No problem. The dry ice doesn't stick, because it's subliming.

P2 **drops the chunk of dry ice into a tall glass flask of water.**

Pretty? And look: I'm not doing a thing! Nature is doing all the "work".

The white cloud is a cloud of tiny water droplets,
formed when the cold front of cold CO_2 vapor in a CO_2 bubble
meets a humid front produced by evaporation of surrounding liquid water into the bubble.

P1 In this large rectangular fish bowl are chunks of dry ice.
By sublimation, they've probably, by now, filled the fish bowl with CO_2 vapor,
denser than air for two reasons:
   CO_2 molecules are *heavier* than air's molecules,
   and the gaseous CO_2 is much *colder* than the surrounding air.

P2 We can demonstrate CO2's density in several ways.

P1 and P2 –

- Invite volunteers to blow soap bubbles into the fish bowl.
- Invite volunteers to inhale, gently, from the fish bowl CO2 vapor, through soda straws. What's it like?
  "Dry pop," some youngsters say.
- Carefully scoop CO2 vapor into a pitcher.
- Carefully pour the pitcher's contents into a glass (to snickers, sometimes).
- Finally: Pour the glass's contents over a burning candle.
  (to clapping, by appreciative audiences).

Playing around with *invisible* gases is good preparation for using the explanatory power of the invisible atoms of an atomic model of matter.
Illustrated is the role of imagination in the science of atoms and molecules.

Volunteers, in attempts to repeat the CO2 pours, often fail, at first, for not having been observant. With suggestions from an audience, they generally succeed, eventually, to pleased audiences' applause.

One time, however, the candle didn't go out for a program's principal presenter: a high school chemistry teacher on sabbatical leave to a Van Program, and, now, back in the auditorium of his own high school as a program's principal presenter. What to do? Remember: *There's always a reason for everything.* Nature always does her thing.

The candle's flame was flickering. A draft? A glance sideways revealed what appeared to be a large air-return for an air-handling system. Pour the CO2 *upwind* of the candle, suggested the audience.
Tried. Success! Cheers!! People love to see minds at work. It's something seldom if ever see in "action movies", chemical magic shows, and ordinary classroom lectures.

Another time the candle didn't go out, reported a student-team, pleased for having discovered before a large audience what had gone "wrong". Their fish bowl had developed a crack in its bottom. Finding out about their cracked "pot" turned out to be the highlight of their "Van Visit".
It showed, wrote a student, that "You scientists aren't cracked pots."

If one goes through life trying promising things, said G. P. Thomson, Nobel Laureate for co-discovery of electron' wave-like character (whose corpuscular character was discovered by his father, also a Nobel Laureate) you have to be very unlucky indeed not to hit on good things every once in a while.

Especially "good things" in programs aimed at bringing before the public approximations to an inductive science are, as said, occurrence of *unexpected events* — especially *questions*, from Nature (in the form of surprising events), and from audiences, owing to curiosity.

"Does your bell jar demo work with methane?" wondered a student.

"Sometimes. But—as you might expect, since methane's molecules are much heavier than hydrogen's molecules, hence, slower-moving—the demo is much *slower*. And there's not always an explosion at the end, as methane's explosion limits are much narrower than those of hydrogen.

Twice one fall the bottle rocket demo didn't proceed as expected.
The first time was at the end of program executed in a church basement with a low ceiling.
Presenters and their audience had adjourned on a crisp fall day to an adjacent parking lot for the bottle rocket demo. However, instead of clearing the church, as expected, the bottle scarcely cleared the end of its launching rod. Presenters left puzzled and disappointed. Had they messed up somehow with the hydrogen peroxide? Or the alcohol?

The second occurrence was a few weeks later in an auditorium on a university campus early one morning for an honors class of high school students. Expected to make it to the back of the auditorium, an alcohol bottle rocket barely made it to the first row of classroom seats, occupied by students in jackets and coats, because the building's central heating system wasn't working. Of course! The hardest things to see sometimes stare one in the face.

Low temperature? Low alcohol vapor pressure. Low vapor pressure? Lean fuel mixture. Lean fuel mixture? Little thrust. Little thrust? Disappointing rocket performance — or so it seemed, at first. Later in the season the lemon became lemonade in the form of a well-received Faraday Christmas Lecture on "The Chemical History of the Bottle Rocket" featuring different fuels at different temperatures.

P1 Scoops CO2 vapor into a bucket and pours its contents down a Plexiglas-sided candle staircase with burning candles on its steps. Silently they go out, one by one.

P2 At 9:30 p.m., August 21, 1986, Lake Nyos, a 200 m deep, highly carbonated African crater lake suddenly erupted, expelling a 50 m thick lethal mist of CO_2 and water droplets that swept down adjacent valleys at a speed of about 20 mph, silently asphyxiating in four villages nearly all villagers and their cattle, together with low-roosting birds.

P1 Pooling of gases, downward and upward in the atmosphere, follows directly, by Avogadro's Law, from the relative masses of their molecules.

Relative Masses of Some Atoms and Molecules		
H 1	H_2 2	CH_4 16
He 4	N_2 28	C_3H_8 44
C 12	O_2 32	$(C_2H_5)_2O$ 94
N 14	H_2O 18	C_8H_{18} 144
O 16	CO_2 44	

P2 Pooling upward are hydrogen, helium, and methane.
Pooling downward are CO_2, propane (C_3H_8), and vapors of diethyl ether and octane.

P1 Molecules of CO_2 and propane have essentially the same mass.
Although the two substances have entirely different *chemical* properties
(Propane fuels ordinary fires, whereas carbon dioxide extinguishes ordinary fires),
their *mechanical* properties, insofar as those depend on molecular mass, are essentially the same.

P2 So, let's try propane down our candle staircase, shall we? Stand by with fire extinguishers.
We'll use one lit candle, at the bottom of the staircase.

P1 collects propane from a propane torch inverted in a bucket located below and at safe distance from flames.

P1 pours propane down the candle staircase.
For a moment nothing seems to happen, then -

WHOOSH!

"Do it again!" shout students.

They can see that, like all our demos, the Propane Pour is an easy demo to do.

"Done differently?"

"With *two* candles."

Same result — followed by dead silence. One can almost feel the disappointment in the room.

But, hey. Observers may have learned something about limiting reagents.

A STUDENT'S QUESTION: "Can you pour methane *up* the candle staircase?"

"It would just go straight up into the air."

"I mean: Can you pour methane up an *inverted* staircase?"

"Great question! Have you thought of becoming a scientist?"

"Come on up on the stage and we'll try it."

"How should we position the staircase?"

"How should we collect the methane?"

"Where should we locate the methane-igniting candle?"

"How are you going to introduce the methane?

The student-questioner pours methane collected in an inverted waste paper basket up into the inverted candle staircase resting on a table on the edges of its Plexiglas sides with its original top step projecting over an edge of the table and with a burning candle perched on an upright two-by-four above the staircase's new top step. After an anxious moment -

WHOOSH!

P1 That's nice: Clapping for Nature when she's done her things for us.

P2 And look at that! The staircase walls have fogged up. Shades of our bell jar.
There must be hydrogen in methane.

P1 Methane is, in fact, weight-wise and atom-wise, Nature's most hydrogen-rich compound.

P2 And look at that! The candle's flame, which initiated the big flame, has been extinguished by the flame's rising, hot (hence low density), gaseous combustion products (even though some of its molecules are relatively heavy CO_2 molecules).

P2 "Nothing can live on its own wastes."
And candles and methane burn in air to the same wastes.
What puts out one flame puts out the other flame.

A HIGHLY PRACTICAL PRINCIPLE OF FIRE EXTINCTION

Most fires produce the same wastes.

Carbon Dioxide and Water

The usual choices for smothering fires

P1 Grease fires are an exceptional situation, considered later.

P2 Most of the following facts follow largely from the following list's second or third statement, cited to illustrate — with the rest of this program — the explanatory power of the kinetic-molecular model of matter, especially applied to gases.

Unlike solids and liquids, gases -

o   Are soft
o   Are chiefly empty space
o   Have large free volumes
o   Have very low densities
o   Have no tensile strength
o   Have very low viscosities
o   Are poor conductors of heat
o   Do not give diffraction patterns
o   Expand and fill the available space
o   Are all poor conductors of electricity
o   Mix with each other in all proportions
o   Have high, nearly identical compressibilities
o   Have high, nearly identical thermal expansions
o   Are often impossible to see with the naked eye
o   Are never composed of long, polymeric molecules
o   Propagate light with nearly the speed of a vacuum
o   Have high numerical measures of molecular disorder
o   Do not exist at temperatures close to absolute zero
o   Have nearly the same "equation of state": PV = nRT
o   Do not have collective modes of molecular oscillations
o   Offer molecules virtually complete freedom of rotation
o   Are often shipped at high pressure in heavy steel tanks
o   Are responsible for the mechanical violence of explosions
o   Are the most stable form of matter at high temperatures
o   Are the most stable form of matter at very low pressures
o   Exhibit the phenomenon of condensation on being cooled
o   Are sometimes shipped at cryogenic temperatures as liquids
o   Have distinct entropies of translation, rotation, and vibration
o   Are the least stable form of matter at very low temperatures
o   Are the state of matter fuel and oxidizer must be in to yield flames
o   Gave rise to a special branch of chemistry called "Pneumatic Chemistry"
o   Propagate sound, by way of molecule-molecule collisions, relatively slowly
o   Require special "gas handling equipment" for their manipulation in laboratories
o   Offer relatively little resistance to passage of rays from radioactive substances
o   Played an important role in the development of the kinetic-molecular model of matter
o   Received their generic name, gas, relatively late in the development of scientific thought
o   Have molecule-molecule collision frequencies that are sharply dependent on the sizes of molecules
o   Offer molecules path lengths between collisions that are much greater than molecular dimensions
o   Were often overlooked as reactants or products of chemical reactions in the early history of chemistry
o   Have, at the same temperature and pressure, approximately the same number of molecules per unit volume

P2 We'll leave the slide up for several moments for you to scan while we check out the rest of our equipment.

P1 The molecular model of matter is useful in understanding substances' large increases in volume on sublimation and vaporization at ordinary pressures.

P1 **places several ounces of crushed dry ice in a pop bottle, caps it with a balloon, and sets it aside for observation.**

P2 **points to a beaker of boiling water** and says:
"To boil that beaker dry would require production of a huge volume of water vapor, as bubbles filled with water vapor."

P1 Here's another instance of the same phenomenal increase in volume, owing to formation of a gas.

P1 **pours vinegar into a small beaker, adds liquid soap, and then pours the contents into a large beaker containing baking soda.**

P2 We can reverse that increase in volume by lowering the gas's temperature.
All molecules are sticky to some degree, especially molecules of water.
The temperature at which dew forms is called the "dew point".
In humid weather water molecules in air may condense on glasses containing cold drinks.
-78 °C is sufficiently cold to cause CO_2 molecules to stick together at atmospheric pressure, as dry ice.

P1 Even nitrogen molecules stick together, as a liquid, at atmospheric pressure, at – 196 °C, as in this Dewar.

P1 **pours liquid nitrogen from a large Dewar onto the floor, onto an empty table, into a beaker, and into a wide-mouth Dewar,** and says:
"The white wispy clouds are little droplets of condensed water vapor."

P2 Three kinds of substances are interesting to cool down with liquid nitrogen:
- rubbery substances (composed of long, tangled, flexible molecules), above their glass-transition temperatures
- substances with a high water content (which will freeze), such as flowers, fruits, and vegetables
- gases

A pencil? Not so much.

P2 **dips a pencil into liquid nitrogen and then grasps it with his or her hand.**

P1 **stretches an uninflated balloon, cools it with LN2, and crushes it by hand.**

P2 **pounds a nail into a board with a liquid-nitrogen-cooled banana.**

P1 **has a volunteer smash a liquid-nitrogen cooled hollow rubber ball against the floor, with distribution to the audience of pieces of the shattered ball.**

P2 **has a volunteer sniff a flower** (Any odor? "Yes."), then cool it with LN2\- (Any odor? "No.), and, finally, **crush it by hand.**

"May I put my finger in the liquid nitrogen?" asks a student.
"We're always told not to," replies P2. But if you do it like this, well, o.k."

P2 **dips a finger quickly in and out of LN2.**

Student follows suit, examines withdrawn finger, and says: "Hm. Dry water."

P2 Dipping a warm finger into liquid nitrogen is like dipping a red hot poker into liquid water. Vaporization of the liquid prevents the dipped object from getting wet.

P1 **in a darkened room squeezes from a wash bottle several drops of water onto a red hot spoon.** The liquid floats on a jacket of steam, like an air puck, or like droplets of LN2 on the floor or a table top, until suddenly it wets the hot spoon and flash evaporates.

P2 **cools a methane-filled balloon slightly, until it ceases to levitate, barely; places it on the floor; and suggests that the audience pretend that it is urging the balloon to levitate.**

Young children go bonkers when the balloon levitates, on its own, it seems, even if they've seen the balloon cooled. Heat conduction is invisible to the naked eye.

Teachers and parents say that their kids believe that their visiting scientists are magicians. Is it worthwhile, one wonders, to go to the trouble of attempting to present for youngsters something that approaches authentic science if they believe that their presenters are merely magicians?

"Do you do parties?" wondered a parent. Or shopping malls, wondered a director of a university's outreach initiatives. No. Been there, tried that. Our conclusion? Science is a sacred enterprise, worthy of serious settings, such as schools, colleges and universities, civic theaters, churches, and such.

P1 **tests with a burning splint the vapors in the beaker above boiling LN2** and remarks that, at the low temperature of the vapors, 77 K, compared to about 300 K for room temperature, the cold nitrogen vapors are denser than room-temperature CO_2.

P1 **pours 77 K nitrogen vapors in a bucket down the candle staircase.**

P2 **blows up a balloon, cools it with LN2 in a dish pan until it collapse, cuts it with scissors over a beaker, and tests the beaker's gaseous contents with a burning splint.** At first it goes out, as predominantly nitrogen boils off. Later it yields the classic test for oxygen.

P1 **repeats cooling of a methane-filled balloon with LN2, until it collapses.**

Enhanced evaporation of our liquid nitrogen coolant signals that the methane is condensing, with liberation of its heat of condensation.

P1 **cuts the balloon with scissors over a beaker of water.**

P2 **quickly places a flaming torch, horizontal, on the table adjacent to the beaker where it can ignite downward pooling cold methane vapors spilling, unseen, out of the beaker.**

P1 **picks up the beaker and its contents, walks out into the audience,** and says:

- The liquid methane is floating on the water. It's Nature's lightest oil.
- Oil and water don't mix.
- Methane has gone by condensation from the gaseous to the liquid state and by vaporization back to the gaseous state and, now, is burning.
- The dark space in the beaker above the surface of the water and beneath the lower flame front is cold methane vapor of a diffusion flame.
- Forming beneath the liquid methane is a white solid: ordinary ice, which quickly melts once all the liquid methane has evaporated.
- In short order we've witnessed four changes of state and a chemical reaction.

P2 While we're in the business of condensing gases with liquid nitrogen, watch this:

P2 **pours liquid nitrogen into a kitchen sauce pan, walks to the center aisle, holds up the pan up for all to see, and lowers it for those nearby to see into it.**

P2 The outside of the pan has, now, become sufficiently cold to condense water vapor from the air, as frost, up to the level of the liquid nitrogen inside the pan.
And, hey! What's this?
The frost looks *wet!* Liquid water? At liquid nitrogen temperatures? Hardly.
Now there's a liquid dripping from the pan.
Catch a drop? What does it feel like?
"It stings?"
Because it's really hot? Or because it's extremely cold?
We're liquefying air!
Let's see if we can collect some of it, more speedily,
by inverting the arrangement of our event's principal participants.

P1 **floats the kitchen pan, empty, in liquid nitrogen in a plastic dish pan.** Collected inside the pan after several minutes are ten milliliters or so of a liquid, **poured into a 500 mL beaker and tested, repeatedly, by a volunteer, with a splint.**

P1 At first the splint goes out (as once before), surrounded by particularly volatile, nitrogen-rich air. Later it glows brilliantly (as once before), surrounded by less volatile, oxygen-rich air.

BACK STORY TO THE PAN-IN-LIQUID-NITROGEN DEMO. A colleague, Dr. Garry Warnock, active in Pittsburgh's "Van Program" (named for its most visible physical feature) was playing around one afternoon around 1991 in his office with a torpedo-shaped magnet dropped down copper, aluminum, and stainless steel tubes, with times of descent noted. Thinking to increase that time by increasing induced currents by decreasing the metals' electrical resistances by cooling the tubes, we stoppered one end of a tube and poured liquid nitrogen into the other end. That's when we notice the bottom of the tube frosting up, and turning wet.

P2 The beauty of an oxygen-enhanced flame is its luminosity.

P1 Most luminosity of luminous flames arises from the presence in them of *hot solid particles*.

P2 **places a spatula across the tip of a candle's flame for a few seconds, then holds up the spatula for all to see.**
Evidently there's carbon in candle wax.

The black spot is commonly called "soot", or "carbon black", the chief ingredient of printers' toners.

Carbon is present in the flame, as a solid.
Its melting point is thousands of degrees above a candle's flame temperature.

This demo, and the ones about the physics and chemistry of the candle that follow it are from Michael Faraday's public lecture "On the Chemical History of a Candle". They're the epitome of simple, short, safe, inexpensive, easily explained demos, of interest to almost anyone with a child-like curiosity about how the world works, and executable at home, at a dinner table, say, should conversation lag.

AN ASIDE ABOUT FARADAY. A scientist has finally made it, professionally, it's been said, when his or her name moves from books' author indices to their subject indices. By that measure Michael Faraday is, arguably, the greatest scientist who ever lived.

Faraday may not be the most famous scientist who ever lived, but, as the father of the physics of electricity in motion, he is, for mankind, arguably the world's most important scientist who ever lived. Einstein's name, e.g., or a derivative of it, appears in the *American Heritage Dictionary of the English Language* <u>two</u> times, as **Einstein** and **einsteinium**. For **Newton** the number is <u>three</u>: **Newton** (mathematician and scientist), **Newton** (city names), and **newton** (a unit of force). For Faraday it is <u>six!</u>: **Faraday** (British physicist and chemist, 1791-1867), **Faraday effect**, **faradic**, **faradism**, **faradization**, and **faradize**.

From the time he was a young man Faraday spent his life at the Royal Institution in England, where he pursued pure and applied research in physics and chemistry and delivered public lectures, among them his favorite: Christmas Lectures on "The Chemical History of the Candle for Juvenile Audiences."

When Faraday demonstrated in one of his public lectures mankind's first electric motor, consisting of a short, thin wire mounted nearly vertically in a magnetic field with its lower free to rotate in a circle in a pool of mercury in a small dish when an electric current was passed through the wire, Britain's prime minister provoked Faraday with the question: "What's the use of *that*?" "Sir," replied Faraday, "someday you may tax it."

Through diligent, thoughtful practice Faraday became a "prince of demonstrators."
He prefaced his demonstration-lectures on a candle with these remarks:

> **"I propose to bring before you, in the course of these lectures, the Chemical history of the candle. There is not a law under which any part of the universe is governed which does not come into play and is touched upon in these phenomena. There is no more open door by which you can enter into the study of natural philosophy than by considering the phenomena of a candle."**

P2 **places his spatula for a few seconds immediately above the candle's wick.**

Ah, as expected, for a diffusion flame: a *soot ring*.
Combustionwise, a candle's flame — like all diffusion flames — is hollow.
Its vaporized fuel obtains its oxygen for combustion by diffusion into the surrounding air.
There's no air, hence no combustion, immediately around the wick,
only wax vapor, from solid wax that has melted, wicked up the wick, and vaporized.

P2 **examines his soot ring closely. Tilts it at different angles.**
I see evidence of condensed wax vapor, in the form of a thin film,
colored like oil on a wet pavement.
Check me out.

P2 **and the team pass spatulas with soot rings on them to members of the audience.**

P1 We might have anticipated that a candle's flame is hollow, from its wick's shape and colors, and the Firemen's Triangle of Fire.

The following sequence of observations and conclusions illustrate what Faraday's close personal friend William Whewell called in his famous *Philosophy of the Inductive Sciences* "The Fundamental Antithesis of Science", between things and thoughts.

Evidence (E) and Inferences (I) Based on the Shape and Colors of a Candle's Wick

- E: The wick, black over most of its exposed length, is orange at its tip.
- I: The wick is hot — orange hot — at its tip.
- E: The wick is burning at its tip.
- I: The wick is combustible — a potential fuel for fire.
- E: The wick is not burning inside the visible flame.
- I: The portion of the wick inside the flame is, nonetheless, probably hot.
- I: Something other than fuel and heat is missing from the Triangle of Fire. in the region around the wick.
- I: It must be that there's no air inside the flame, owing to vaporization from the wick of wicked up candle wax.

P2 Here, on a larger scale, is the Candle Wick Phenomenon.

P2 **pours drug-store alcohol into a 500 mL beaker; adds water to give about a 50-50 mixture of alcohol and water** "to cool down our flame" (usually not absolutely necessary); **soaks a towel in the mixture** "being certain not to leave dry spots;" **wrings out the towel;** *dries hands;* **dons a fire-proof glove; has lights turned off; holds the towel by tongs over a flame for a moment; swings the towel about,** perhaps in circles and figure eights, "to lessen heating of my glove"; **removes glove; picks up the towel** "It's just pleasantly warm;" **folds towel and wipes face** "as one might do riding first class on a plane"; **holds up the towel for the audience to see that** "It's not even singed;" **and tosses it to the audience.**

A Nonburning "Nonburning Towel. One time during an evening program at a university in western North Carolina, the nonburning towel-demo didn't proceed as expected. After immersion in alcohol — provided, with the towel, by the University's department of chemistry — and exposure to a burning match, struck and held by a young lady in the first row of desks, *there was no flame at the towel!* Was the water-diluted "alcohol" really alcoholic? A small amount poured into a cake pan and torched burned with alcohol's characteristic, almost sootless blue flame. "Let's try the experiment with your demonstrator's handkerchief. There we are. What we expected. No surprise. So what's going on with this towel?"

Up went a hand at the back of the room where the faculty was seated. "Our lowest bidder for supplying towels this year was the State Prison. *Their towels are terrible.* I believe they must be polypropylene, or something like that."

Sure enough. Where a volunteer had held a match to the bottom corner of the towel, *the towel had melted,* a bit. Heated cotton doesn't melt. It chars. But polyethylene and similar polymers do melt. Also, hydrogen-bonded water and alcohol don't wet oil, polyethylene, and similar polymers. It was the unexpected highlight and most memorable moment of the program: finding out why the "Non-Burning Towel Demo" surprised us. Now, years later, the demonstrator remembers little else about that evening.

As P1 holds up a candle for the audience, and TV cameras, to see,
P2 place across the tip of the candle's flame a 4x4 inch square of metal screen.

P2 As expected: rising black smoke? Composed of what? Soot?

P2 **places the screen across the flame immediately above the wick.**

P2 Ah. A hollow flame. And rising *white* smoke.

P1 One might think we were electing a Pope.

P2 What's the white smoke composed of?
Combustible particles of condensed wax vapor?

P2 **holds the candle. P1 lights a match with it. P2 blows out the candle. P1 places the burning match in the rising white smoke, a bit above the wick.**

P2 A striking strike-back, if we do say so.

P1 We need another volunteer, perhaps someone contemplating a career in the theatre.

P1 Your name? Jack? Are you hungry Jack?
Humor us, if you would, by coming up on the stage for this energy bar.
Umwrapping it. And munching on it for a bit.

Jack is illustrating for us why we have feet and legs, hands and arms, eyes, and, for limb-eye coordination, a central nervous system, in order to secure food.

And now Jack is showing us why we have teeth and jaws,
to prepare our food for digestion for transport to cells of our bodies' organs.
Thank you, Jack. Are you breathless after all that? No?

Even so, Jack was using his lungs, to secure oxygen-containing air,
for transport via iron atoms in hemoglobin of his blood
pumped by his heart through arteries and thence to his organs' cells
for collision with food-derived molecules to maintain his Fires of Life
that, to burn at life-sustaining rates,
require a flame temperature, so to speak, of about 98.6 °F.

98.6 Degrees Fahrenheit

To maintain our bodies near 98.6 °F,
we eat food, wear clothing, and live in houses.
To pay for food, clothing, and shelter,
we have jobs.
To have good jobs, we go to school.
To get to jobs, we drive cars.
To fuel our cars, we buy gasoline.
To manufacture gasoline, we import oil.
To secure sources of oil, we have armed forces,
foreign policy, and a large federal government.
To support the government, we pay taxes,
to support enforcement of our foreign policy,
to secure sources of oil,
for manufacture of gasoline,
to run our cars,
to get to work,
to earn money,
to pay for food, clothing, and shelter,
to maintain our bodies near 98.6 °F.

P2 It's a Chemist's World View.
Now, back to our candle.
Its appeal lies in its luminosity.
One of Nature's most luminous flames is used in flares.

P1 CAUTION. The magnesium-oxygen flame you are about to see is so hot it radiates significant energy in the ultraviolet. It's best not to look at it directly for more than a few moments.

P1 **torches a tong-held strip of magnesium.**

P1 A diffusion flame? Hence hollow?
Solid magnesium, our fuel, and its oxidizer, oxygen of air, weren't premixed.
Air's oxygen does not dissolve in solid magnesium.
To complete the triangle of fire, the magnesium metal must have "dissolved" in the air,
 so to speak; i.e., it must have vaporized.

P2 Magnesium has, in fact, the lowest boiling point of all the metals,
after the "volatile metals" zinc, cadmium, and mercury, which, however, are poor fuels for brilliant flames because they haven't nearly the affinity for oxygen that magnesium has.

P1 Mercuric oxide was, in fact, an early source of oxygen.

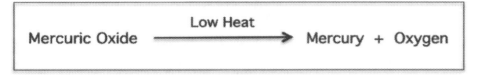

We'd show you the reaction but for one reason, if I can remember it.

P2 Mercury vapor is highly toxic. It causes, among other harmful things, loss of memory.

P1 Thanks for the reminder. Now back to our magnesium.
It's easy to test for magnesium vapor in magnesium's flame.

P1 **brushes a spatula against a magnesium flame for a few moments,
in two places: at the spatula's tip and slightly back from its tip.**

P1 Black spots! Condensed magnesium vapor? Let's try a "confirmatory test".

P1 **dips the tip of the spatula into hydrochloric acid. "The acid test."**

P2 The outer black spot vanishes, with formation of little bubbles, of hydrogen, –

A FAMOUS CHEMICAL REACTION

Acid + Active Metal = Dihydrogen Gas

P1 **heats the underside of the spatula with a torch.** The inner black spot turns white.

ANOTHER FAMOUS REACTION

Active Metal + Oxygen = Metal Oxide

P1 Magnesium oxide used to be a National Bureau of Standard's standard for whiteness.

P2 Sodium, from a family of Nature's most active metals, the alkali metals, releases hydrogen from even an acid as weak as water.

P2 prepares to add sodium to water, by cutting a small piece from a chunk of it.

P2 Sodium has only one bonding electron per atom.
Consequently, sodium-sodium bonds of metallic sodium are weak.
The metal is so soft one can cut it with a spatula's blade.

P1 But first two things.

P1 adds a few drops of phenolphthalein to water in a Petri dish resting on an overhead projector and checks the water's electrical conductivity with a light bulb in series with two electrodes across 110 volts. The light bulb doesn't light up.

P2 drops a small piece of sodium into the Petri dish and prepares to make observations and to draw inferences.

SODIUM AND WATER
Evidence *and Inductions*

- The sodium floats! *It's less dense than water.*
- Sodium's cross-section is circular*! It's melted. The reaction is exothermic.*
- The sodium is moving. *It seems to be propelled by an invisible gas.*

- Can the gas be trapped? Yes, with agility, with an inverted test tube.
- "Pop" goes the gas, exposed to a flame. *It seems to be hydrogen: colorless, less dense than air, and flammable.*

- Trailing the sodium is a pink streak. *The solution is turning basic.*

- Loss of protons of H_2 molecules by H_2O suggests *formation of OH- ions.*
- Loss of electrons of H_2 molecules by Na suggests *formation of Na+ ions.*

- The solution has become a conductor of electricity. *It contains ions.*
- The sodium has disappeared. *Sodium is a reactant.*

Observations suggest this model:

$$2\ Na(s)\ +\ 2\ H_2O(l)\ =\ 2\ Na^+(aq)\ +\ 2\ OH^-(aq)\ +\ H_2(g)\ +\ Heat$$

P1 Here's another instance of chemical thought.

OXYGEN AFFINITIES OF MAGNESIUM, CARBON, AND HYDROGEN

- A magnesium flame is white hot owing to the presence of hot solid MgO.
- A candle flame is yellow hot owing to the presence of hot solid carbon.
- Flame temperatures can be judged by the colors of their black body radiation.
- White hot is hotter than yellow hot which is hotter than cherry red.
- CONCLUSION 1: a magnesium flame is hotter than a candle flame.
- CONCLUSION 2: Mg has a greater affinity for oxygen than do C and H.
- INFERENCE 1: Oxygen, given a choice, reacts with Mg rather than with C or H.
- INFERENCE 2: If O is already attached to C or H, Mg, if hot, may remove it.
- CO_2 and H_2O contain oxygen and are, therefore, potential oxygen atom donors.
- INFERENCE 3: **Mg burning in air may continue to burn in gaseous CO_2 and H_2O.**

P1 **checks the gas above boiling water in a beaker with a burning splint to see if all air has been purged from the beaker,** and says, as the splint goes out:

"Wood doesn't burn in steam."

P2 That's an instance of everyday, practical, chemical knowledge that just about everybody knows.

P1 Indeed, since every *thing* is made of atoms and molecules, and nothing else,
and since chemistry is the science of atoms and molecules,
chemistry is, on its practical side, "The Familiar Science".

P2 **holds a strip of burning magnesium in the steam above the boiling water.**
It continues to burn, with some sputtering.

P1 **adds vinegar to baking soda in a beaker, checks with a burning splint for the presence of carbon dioxide,** and says, as the splint goes out,

"Wood doesn't burn in carbon dioxide".

P2 **then holds a strip of burning magnesium in the CO2-containing beaker.**
The magnesium continues to burn.

P1 I see black specks. That's consistent with the equation –

$$2\ Mg(s)\ +\ CO_2(g)\ =\ 2\ MgO(s)\ +\ C(s,\ black)$$

P2 Here's a more striking execution of that reaction.

P2 **places magnesium turnings in a golf-ball-sized cavity gouged with a screwdriver in the center of thick slab of dry ice resting on a large metal sheet behind an explosion shield; torches the turnings (perhaps blowing on them slightly); lays a similar slab of dry ice on top of the first slab; and steps back to watch, lights down. While the assembly is still glowing, P2 picks it up, wearing heavy gloves, and walks out into the audience to show them a golf-ball-sized sphere of magnesium-oxide-covered black carbon.**

41

Virtues of the Magnesium/Dry-Ice Demonstration-Experiment

- It's a simple, short, safe, inexpensive, easily executed, striking visual event.

- Visible are all reactants (metallic magnesium, dry ice) and all products (white magnesium oxide and black carbon).

- A correct chemical equation for the event is, as has been noted, easily written.

$$2\ Mg(s)\ +\ CO_2(g)\ =\ 2\ MgO(s)\ +\ C(s,\ black)$$

P1 Each element's symbol stands for an atom, or, if one likes, a mole of atoms; i.e., a gram formula weight of the element.

P2 The chemical equation illustrates –

A FUNDAMENTAL CHEMICAL PRINCIPLE

Atoms are conserved in chemical transformations of matter.

What goes in must come out or pile up.

P1 The Atom-Conservation Principle has several practical consequences.

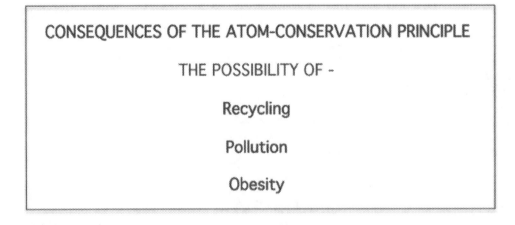

P2 Plant and animal life is recycling on a grand scale.

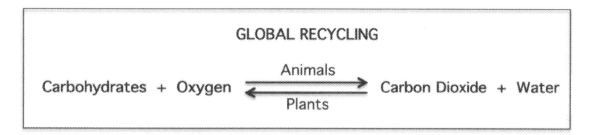

GLOBAL RECYCLING

Carbohydrates + Oxygen ⇄ (Animals / Plants) Carbon Dioxide + Water

P1 Often overlooked are *invisible* pollutants, such as atmospheric CO2. And methane, whose many infrared-active vibration frequencies are many times more planet-warming through a greenhouse phenomenon than are carbon dioxide molecules, which have only one, highly active planet-warming vibration.

"Out of sight, out of mind."

P2 Not invisible in its effects on fish is lake and river water used to condense low-pressure steam exiting steam turbines at electric-power-producing plants.

THERMAL POLLUTION

- *High-temperature, high-pressure steam* at a power plant is useless, for production of mechanical effects (such as rotation of turbine blades of an electricity-generating generator), in the absence of a *pressure-difference*, created by a *lower-temperature, steam-condensing condenser*.

- Steam condensing is an exothermic, heat-releasing event.

- To facilitate cooling of steam-condensing condensers, power plants are often located near rivers or lakes.

- The temperature of the adjacent body of water rises.

- Fish are cold-blooded. Their bodies adopt the temperatures of their surroundings.

- Rises in body temperature increase rates of fishes' biochemical reactions.

- Faster metabolizing fish need more oxygen.

- But gases are less soluble in hot water than in cold water.

  [Solution of a gas in water is, like liquefaction of the gas, an *exothermic* event. Hence, by Le Chatelier's Principle, a rise in temperature decreases gas solubility.]

- Few native American fish can survive temperatures much above 90 °F. They suffocate.

P1 **You can demonstrate the effect of temperature on the solubility of a gas in a liquid by heating air-saturated tap water in a pan.**

The little bubbles that appear on the sides and bottom of the pan well before the water begins to boil are filled with air, less soluble in hot water than in cold water.

P2 We can illustrate the same phenomenon for carbon dioxide in water with dry ice and universal indicator.

P2 adds universal indicator to three tall glass flasks of water with stirring bars resting on magnetic stirrers that are also hot plates, two off, the last one on. To the first one P2 adds, alternately, dilute hydrochloric acid and dilute sodium hydroxide, to show the indicator's color in acidic solution (pink) and basic solution (violet).

FOR STUDENTS OF PHYSICAL CHEMISTRY: Pink means absorption in the high-frequency, high-photon-energy, blue region of the visible spectrum, blue and violet to absorption in the lower-frequency, lower-energy, red-region of the spectrum. "Acidic" means high protonation of photon-absorbing electrons, making their absorption of photons more difficult and, thereby, shifting the absorbed photon's frequencies toward the blue end of the spectrum and rendering transmitted light pink.

P1 drops chunks of dry ice into the two remaining flasks, one cold, one hot. Quickly they turn pink.

P1 Carbon dioxide was once called "carbonic acid gas".

P1 "Oxy-gen" means "acid-generator". Non-acidic carbon united chemically with oxy-gen yields a weak acid: carbonic acid.

P1 Note that the water in the flask on the hot hot plate isn't as pink as the colder water. It has less carbon dioxide dissolved in it.

P1 adds sodium hydroxide to one of the dry-ice-containing flasks. It turns from pink through green to blue and violet, and then back through that sequence of colors to pink.

P2 It's pink again, but not as pink as before. Present is a buffer (a topic for another day).

P1 Another example of oxygen's acid-generating character is its transformation of phosphorus into an acid.

P1 squirts oxygen into a large round bottom flask.

P2 torches a crucible of red phosphorus perched on a graduated cylinder resting in a large crystallizing dish nearly full of water spiked with universal indicator and a few drops of sodium hydroxide, to turn the indicator violet.

P1 immediately inverts the oxygen-containing flask and places it through the ring of a ring stand over the phosphorus-containing pedestal and down into the water of the crystallizing dish until the end of its throat rests on the bottom of the crystallizing dish.

P2 Lights out, please.
That's called "The Phosphorus Moon".
The white "cloud", illuminated by the burning phosphorus at its center,
is smoke: a suspension, in oxygen gas, of solid particles composed of P_4O_{10} molecules,
highly soluble in water.

P1 The water is beginning to rise,
owing to the weight of the atmosphere resting on it,
as combustion consumes the flask's oxygen.

P2 The indicator is turning pink.

P1 Being formed from the action of water on P_4O_{10} is phosphoric acid, H_3PO_4, one of the common oxy-acids.

Common Oxy-Acids of Elements in the p-Block

B	H_3BO_3	Boric Acid.	Very weak acid. Used in eye washes.
C	H_2CO_3	Carbonic Acid.	Weak acid. In tooth-dissolving carbonated drinks.
P	H_3PO_4	Phosphoric Acid.	Fairly strong acid. Many industrial uses.
S	H_2SO_4	Sulfuric Acid.	Strong acid. Industry's most widely used chemical.
Cl	$HClO_4$	Perchloric Acid.	Very strong acid. Powerful oxidizer.

P2 Here's another instance of the dependence of gas solubility on temperature.

P2 **squirts water into a beaker containing dry ice in acetone.**
Produced is a fizzing sound.

P2 The acetone was saturated with CO2 gas at a low temperature, -78 °C, not low enough, however, to freeze the acetone (f.p. -94 °C). Added water quickly froze and liberated its heat of fusion, which warmed the acetone, which degassed, with fizzing.

P1 Next we consider physical changes that played and continue to play major roles in mankind's harnessing the power of fire, and, since WWII, the power of nuclear fission: namely (in both cases), vaporization of water to steam and condensation of steam to liquid water.

P1 **blows up a balloon and ties it off; checks with a splint to see if boiling water in a kitchen sauce pan heated with a hot plate or a torch has purged the pan of air; holds the balloon, as a lid, on the pan, then removes the assembly from its source of heat and sets it aside to cool.**

P2 **repeats the procedure using a lipless glass flask instead of a kitchen pan,** and watches as the balloon expands into the flask as it cools and water vapor condenses, yielding a partial vacuum.

P1 **picks up the pan-and-balloon by the pan's handle and, with the other hand, takes hold of the balloon where it's tied off, at the top.**

P1 **slowly lets go of the pan's handle.**

P1 is hamming it up a bit, the only time a presenter does so.
"Clowns are fun," says a dictionary. Science, however, is serious business.

P1, **holding onto the balloon, gently bobs the pan up and down, then does so more vigorously. Finally P1 swings the pan in a circle** — with care, should it fly free.

P2 **holds up the balloon-and-lipless-flask.** How might we remove the balloon?
Heat the flask?

It was the best of times (an evening with a large, enthusiastic audience of school children, parents, and grandparents in an ancient church in Puerto Rico) and — it might have seemed, for a time, naively, — the worst of times: a simple demo that hadn't proceeded as expected, twice!

"Well, we've seen one thing," said the puzzled demonstrator. 'Nature is lawful.' Things prepared alike behave alike. Twice we've tried to purge this pan of air by boiling water in it, then sealing it with an inflated balloon and letting everything cool. And twice we seemed to have failed to produce an expected partial vacuum in the pan.

"So now I'm going to do something I never do. Instead of *showing* you what has always happened before, I'm going to *tell* you, because I really would like you to try the experiment at home."

Whereupon the demonstrator walked out into the audience and, at one point, raised the pan and balloon over his head for all to see and, holding the balloon tightly against the pan, turned the equipment upside down.

"Hey! Where is that water coming from, that's running down my arm and dripping off my elbow?

"Of course. Of course. Of course. The pan's handle is loose! Where water is running out, around rivets, air had been leaking in."

Afterwards parents and grandparents thanked their guest for the program. "Our kids loved the bottle rockets and cannon," they said. "But the best thing [for homo *sapiens*] was finding out why the balloon-and-pan demo didn't work."

It may be the best way to end a program: Execute the balloon-and-lipless-beaker demo and then challenge an audience to explain why the demo doesn't "work" with a kitchen pan — with a wobbly handle.

P1 Here's another experiment with steam, a flask, a balloon, and the atmosphere,
doing pretty much the same things.

P1 **caps with a balloon an Erlenmeyer flask that's been sitting on a hot plate with a small amount of water in it boiling.** As the flask cools, the balloon pops into it.

P1 **warms the flask over a torch.** The balloon exits the flask.

P1 **sets the assembly aside to cool.**

P2 We can do essentially the same thing with a balloon-capped-dry-ice-containing pop bottle, using as a coolant liquid nitrogen.

P2 **places a balloon-capped-dry-ice-containing pop bottle in a bath of liquid nitrogen, then removes the pop bottle and holds it in a beaker of hot water.**

P1 Here's yet another collapsible container: a can of rectangular cross-section that has a little water boiling in it. (It's a variation of the coke-can demo.)

P2 **checks with a splint to see if the can has been purged of its air.**

P1 **then caps the can tightly and removes it from the heat.**
To speed cooling, P1 sprays the can with a water. The can collapses.

P2 Can we uncollapse the can? By heating it?

P1 **places the collapsed can across a large ring of a ring stand above a burner and stops heating it when it has more or less attained its original shape; then cools it again; &c. — until the can springs a leak at a crease.**

P2 The can's collapse, due to steam's condensation and the weight of the atmosphere,
corresponds to the *power stroke* of mankind's first steam engine,
built by the Englishman Newcomen to raise water from flooded coal mines,
called an "atmospheric engine".

To condense the steam in the power stroke,
Newcomen squirted water into the engine's hot, steam-filled cylinder.

P1 James Watt realized that that was inefficient:
alternately heating a cylinder to the boiling point of water with steam,
then cooling the cylinder with liquid water, to condense the steam.

With a system of valves, Watt connected the working cylinder to a *separate condenser*.
The working cylinder never had to be cooled!
Steam-engine efficiency increased ten-fold!

P2 Steam technology took off. The rest is history:
steam boats, steam shovels, steam engines, steam-driven generators of electricity —
in short, "the industrial revolution".

P1 Here's a container that "collapses" so to speak in a different manner.

P1 **points to a large round bottom flask that has a little water boiling in it.
Resting loosely at its throat is about an 18 inch length of glass tubing through
a one hole stopper. P1 checks with a splint, to see if the flask has been
thoroughly purged of air, then firmly stoppers the flask with the stopper,
removes it from the heat, and inverts it over a large beaker of colored water.**

The glass tubing through the stopper extends about a third of the way into the inverted
flask, supported by the ring of a ring stand. The other end of the glass tubing extends well
into the beaker's water. **To speed cooling of the flask, P1 gives it an alcohol rub.**
Nature, as usual, does the rest: creation, in this instance, of a fountain of water, pushed
upward into the partial vacuum created by the condensing steam by the weight of the
atmosphere above the water in the beaker.

P1 It's called a "steam fountain", or, in its original form, "the miner's friend",
a precursor to Newcomen's "atmospheric engine".
It, too, was used to raise water — as it's now doing — from flooded coal mines. In England
at time of the Industrial Revolution more water was removed from some mines than coal.

P2 Finally, here, behind this explosion shield, we have a special flask for exhibiting water's triple
point: the situation at which all three of water's phases — solid, liquid, and gas — coexist.

P2 **checks with a splint to see if air has been thoroughly purged from a one liter
round bottom flask whose bottom has been heated and, under the influence of
a slight vacuum, induced to bulge *inward*.** The flask contains a boiling chip and boiling
water, to a depth of about an inch above the bulge. Resting loosely at the flask's throat is
(again) a one hole stopper with, this time, a thermometer through it.

P2 **stoppers the flask tightly and, with care, to avoid breaking the thermometer,
inverts the apparatus and places it through the ring of a ring stand.** The tip of
thermometer's bulb is about half an inch below the surface of the water. **To hasten
cooling, P2 pours liquid nitrogen in the inverted flask's depression.**

P2 Water vapor within the flask is condensing. Created is a partial vacuum.
That makes heat-absorbing formation of vapor-filled bubbles — a.k.a. "boiling"; or "internal evaporation" — easier than under a pressure of 1 atmosphere.

P1 The temperature has dropped to 80 degrees Celsius. Yet the water still boils.
It's called "boiling at reduced pressure", or "vacuum distillation".
It's a valuable laboratory technique for purifying by distillation heat-sensitive substances.

Where is this going to end up? We're down to room temperature.
And water is still boiling. Now the thermometer reads about 4 degrees C.
That's the temperature at which liquid water has its maximum density.
Cooled further, it won't sink. But it may freeze.
It *has* frozen, across its surface.
There's a "bump". We've got ice-water boiling!

P2 Present simultaneously are all three states of water: solid, liquid, and vapor,
at a pressure of a fraction of one atmosphere.
We're over 99 percent of the way to a perfect vacuum.
That's the reason for the explosion shield, and our goggles.
There's always the possibility that the flask might implode.

P1 This situation is called "the triple point of water".
Its temperature is *defined*, on the absolute scale, as exactly 273.160000 K (Kelvins),
and, on the Celsius scale, as exactly 0.010000 ºC.

Why exactly 273.16 K?
That makes the difference between water's normal freezing point and its normal boiling point almost exactly 100 K (degrees), as on the old "Centigrade scale".

And why exactly 0.010000 ºC?
That makes water's freezing point on the Celsius scale almost exactly 0.00000 degrees, as on the old Centigrade scale.

P2 The three states of pure water coexist at only one pressure and one temperature.
We have no freedom to choose what T and P are, and have all three phases present.
The system is said to have "zero degrees of freedom".

- -

The Phase Rule
A Riff for Students of General and Physical Chemistry

If we wish to have merely two (not three) states — or "phases" — of water present at the same time, e.g., the liquid and its vapor, say at the chosen temperature of 100 ºC, we can look up in a *Handbook of Chemistry and Physics* to see what the pressure must be: namely, 1 atmosphere, water's so-called "vapor pressure", at 100 ºC.

For two coexisting phases of pure water, we have, it's said, "1 degree of freedom".

For one phase — solid, liquid, or vapor — we have 2 degrees of freedom.

That fact has been called "The Handbook Rule".
To look up a property of liquid water, say its density, in a "Handbook of Chemistry and Physics", we need to have had specified two intensive properties: say T and P.
We are free to choose for any T that we wish to and, within limits, any P

Generalizing, we say, by way of induction, that each increase in the number of phases, P, decreases by unity the number of degrees of freedom, F.

$$F \text{ (for pure water)} = 3 - P$$

If the water is, say, salt water, then one has one more degree of freedom: the concentration of the salt. Generalizing, we say, again by induction, that each increase in the number of components, C, beyond C = 1 (C's value for pure water), increases by unity the number of degrees of freedom.

$$F(\text{impure water}) = 3 - P + (C - 1) = C - P + 2$$

That expression holds for any system of phases and any number of components.
In practice it's used to determine C, by determining P, by observation, and by determining F, by experiment, and then by using the expression -

$$C = F + P - 2$$

Numerical values of C are essential for designing chemical models of chemical systems.

- -

P1 Now, for that question: Our biggest flame?

P2 **places a large piece of paraffin wax in a securely clamped beaker above a Fisher burner resting on sand in a large pan behind an explosion shield. While the wax is melting and warming up to its boiling point,** P1 and P2 prepare for their final demonstration-experiments, by placing buckets of crushed dry ice about the stage and in the orchestra pit and by running methane from a tank into an inverted 55 gallon trash can.

P1 **torches the boiling paraffin wax.**

P2 A grease fire. Extinguished how? With water?

P2 **squirts water from a wash bottle into the grease fire. BIG FLAME.**

P1 Liquid water is denser than liquid paraffin, which, even as a solid, floats in water.

P2 **drops a chunk of paraffin wax into a beaker of water. It floats.**

P1 So our water sank; quickly warmed up in the hot, molten paraffin wax; and boiled, with a huge, grease-atomizing *increase in volume*, by a factor of 1700, the basis of steam technology and modern civilization.

The Factor by which Water Expands on Boiling at its Normal Boiling Point

$$\frac{22.4 \text{ L/mole} (373/273)}{1 \text{ mL/g} \times 18 \text{ g/mole}} = 1700$$

P2 Compare that behavior with the effect of water on an ether fire —
a not uncommon occurrence in chemistry laboratories,
as diethyl ether is extremely volatile. It boils at 34 °C.

P2 squirts water into an ether fire.
    The water sank. Period. Its temperature never came close to 100 °C.

P1 Now, for our largest flame: methane in that barrel, to be poured upward into a flame.
    A safe to do? A big flame sent to the ceiling?
    With its hot combustion products: H_2O and CO_2?
    And excess dinitrogen?

P2 They're all fire-extinguishers!
    Yet it is possible to start a fire with, say, hot steam, this way:

Steam from a steam-generator — a flask of boiling water — passes through copper coils heated by a burner and emerges aimed at a vertical, stiff sheet of paper.

The paper, being combustible, and hot, and exposed to oxygen-containing air on its side *opposite* the jet of superheated steam, catches fire on that side.

P1 Hot is hot. Any hot molecules would have done the same thing.

P2 Experience suggests, however, that in our proposed experiment
combustible surfaces immediately above our ceiling won't come close to their kindling temperatures.

P1 takes up a position in the orchestra pit with the inverted barrel of methane.
    "Hey. This is barrel is sort of light. Just kidding."

P2 takes up a position on the stage with a propane torch taped to a long pole.

P1 I'm concerned, a bit, about one thing.
    Methane from this barrel might enter the torch's air intakes
    and extinguish the torch's flame before it ignites the methane. It's happened.
    Angling the torch's flame downward might prevent that flame-extinction event from occurring.

P2 Do we need to protect our ears?

P1 It'll just be a diffusion flame.

P2 turns the inverted barrel upright. Nature takes over. BIG FLAME.

P1 Combustion!
    One of mankind's best friends.
    Modern chemistry sprang from efforts to understand it.
    Modern civilization heats with it. And harnesses it to do useful work,
    particularly in transportation, through use of internal combustions engines.

P2 Man(un)kind's first internal combustion engine was the cannon.
    We've brought one with us.
    We'll use the same fuel that cars use.

P2 charges with oxygen a cannon barrel sealed off at its lower end with a sturdy cap through which runs a spark plug; adds from a dropper a squirt of isooctane; seals off the top end of the barrel with a tennis ball; rocks the cannon, mounted on wheels, end-to-end, to mix dense octane vapors with oxygen molecules; aims the cannon away from the audience, at a large cardboard box;

and drapes a folded bath towel over the end of the cannon, to slow down the cannon ball.

P1 places ear muffs around his neck; tests the spark of a Tesla coil by bringing its tip close to a ring stand; mentions that a 1 cm spark corresponds to a voltage of some thirty thousand volts; grabs the business end of the Tesla coil with one hand and picks up a fluorescent bulb with the other hand (illustrating, thereby, a property of the high voltage generation); asks two volunteers, provided with ear muffs, to note the cannon's recoil; warns the audience to protect its ears; adjusts his own ear muffs; and sparks the spark plug.

BOOM!

P1 Where's our cannon ball? Inside the box? It's slightly singed.

P1 tosses the "cannon ball" to the audience.

P2 (addressing volunteers): How fast would you say the cannon recoiled before friction brought it to rest? About the speed of a slow walk? Between 1 and 2 miles per hour?
Say 1.5 mph?
How heavy would you say the cannon is? About 15 pounds?
And the mass of the cannon ball? About 1.5 ounces? (I've weighed it.)
Since the cannon and cannon ball were initially at rest, we may say that -

---

By the Conservation of Linear Momentum
(b = cannon ball, c = cannon)

$$m_b v_b + m_c v_c = 0$$
$$\rightarrow$$

$$v_b = - v_c \times (m_c/m_b) \approx - (-1.5 \text{ mph}) \times (15 \times 16 / 1.5) = 240 \text{ mph}$$

P1 That's swift, more than twice as fast as a power pitcher's fast ball.
Holds up the towel: it has a pair of holes in it.

P2 Perhaps this is a good place to stop, before we inflict additional damage on our equipment.

P1 Thanks for coming.

P2 *One announcement for young members of the audience:*

We plan to add hot water to the dry-ice containing red buckets,
to show what happens when humid fronts meet cold fronts.
You're welcome to sit in circles *around* the buckets.
It's best, however, not to put your hands *in* the buckets.
Hot water might scald them. Dry ice might cause frostbite.

Postscript

The previous script describes rather more demos than a visiting team can execute in one class period. In visits to schools Van Teams usually requested double periods, over principals' doubts, however, as to whether or not they could hold students' attention for that length of time. One time at a private parochial elementary school the principal was comfortable allowing a visiting team to continue for three periods. Afterwards one of her students wrote in a thank you note that "The only thing I didn't like was that the program was too short. If it had lasted all day it would be a lot better."

Teaching from demonstration-experiments satisfies Lavoisier's precept: Introduce no term or concept unless there is a need for it based on an experiment or an observation. Accordingly, we ask ourselves in planning public presentations for newcomers to chemistry not "What can we say?" but, rather: "What can we *show*?" Then and only then do we consider what we might say by way of linking demonstrations of Nature's nature into coherent and memorable stories.

Teaching from demonstration-experiments also satisfies a precept of a famous philosopher, mathematician, and educator, Alfred North Whitehead. Your principle goal as a teacher, he wrote in his classic "Aims of Education", is to exhibit yourself In your own true trade: if a chemist, mixing and heating pure substances and designing kinetic-molecular models to account for the results. Doing so for public presentations is, actually, not as difficult to do as it might seem at first. In fact, in one sense it's easy, if, in the same sense, difficult. For as professor Larry Strong liked to say: "Any demo in chemistry illustrates all of chemistry." The difficult thing to do, therefore, is to decide among many attractive alternatives what to do and to say next. Professor Gil Haight had an answer.

"I illustrate all of chemistry with H2 plus O2 yields H2O" Gil liked to say. From there one can pass easily to explosions and explosion limits; distinctive chemical and physical properties of hydrogen and oxygen; combustion; exothermic reactions; Collision Theory, The Triangles of Fire, Life, and Chemistry; elements' critical temperatures; intermolecular forces; activation energies; reaction mechanisms; the First and Second Laws of Thermodynamics; oxidations and reductions; chemical stoichiometry, harnessing the power of fire; the Engineer's Theorem; internal and external combustion engines; the hydrogen economy; and so forth.

To paraphrase Faraday: There is not a law under which any part of chemistry is governed which does not come into play in teaching chemistry from demonstration-experiments featuring Flames and Explosions and The Big Three: Flammable Gases, Liquid Nitrogen, and Dry Ice, plus The Kinetic-Molecular Model of Matter.

APPENDICES

Handouts Concerning the Content and Philosophy of Programs that Feature
Execution, Description, and Explanation of Demonstration-Experiments
with Flammable Gases, Liquid Nitrogen, and Dry Ice

The Gas Laws

V = volume P = pressure T = ideal gas temperature n = amount*

* a.k.a. **population** (of entities: atoms, molecules, protons, electrons, etc.)

Boyle's Law:	V = constant/P	T & n constant
Charles Law:	V = constant x T	P & n constant
Extensive Law:	V = constant x n	T & P constant

Avogadro's Law: $V' = V''$ $T' = T''$ $P' = P''$ $\rightarrow$ $n' = n''$

Consider a volume of gas V' and amount n' at a pressure P' and a temperature T'.

According to the Gas Laws, what is the volume V'' for an amount n'' of the same gas at a pressure P'' and a temperature T''? Answer:

$$V'' = \{[(V' \quad x \quad P'/P'') \quad x \quad T''/T'] \quad x \quad n''/n'\}$$

          Boyle's Law   Charles' Law   Extensive Law

Therefore: $P'' V''/n'' T'' = P' V'/n' T'$

   For gas 1: $(PV/nT)_1$ = constant, say C_1

   For gas 2: $(PV/nT)_2$ = constant, say C_2

Suppose $V_2 = V_1$, $P_2 = P_1$, and $T_2 = T_1$. Then, according to Avogadro's Law, $n_2 = n_1$.

Hence $C_1 = C_2$ = "a universal gas constant", say R (= PV/nT) $\rightarrow$

$$PV = nRT$$

The "Extensive Law" applies to *all substances,* solid, liquid, or gaseous. It might be called "The Zeroth Law" of Atomic Theory, too obvious to be articulated? Perhaps not. A number of modern textbooks of general chemistry refer to the expression V = constant x n (T and P constant) as "Avogadro's Law"! Their "derivations" of the expression $PV = nRT$ from the generalizations of Boyle and Charles and the law of "common sense" V = constant x n (T & P constant) are, accordingly, incomplete.

Generally, too, "derivations" of $PV = nRT$ are unsatisfactory in yet another sense, in stating that Charles *showed* that V(ideal gas) is proportional to "T". That statement gets the logic of the situation exactly backwards. What Charles (and Dalton and others) showed was that *the volume of an ideal gas* (at constant temperature and pressure) *can be used to establish a universal gas temperature scale*, the ideal gas temperature scale, which turns out to be proportional to the thermodynamic absolute temperature scale. The constant of proportionality for the two temperature scales is set, by convention, equal to 1: T(idea gas scale) = T(thermodynamic absolute scale) = T (expressed in "Kelvins").

Pressure of an Ideal Gas According to Kinetic Molecular Theory
$$P = (1/3)nMv^2/V$$

Imagine a collection of n molecules of total mass m and, thus, of mass per molecule $m/n = M$ ("molar mass") bouncing back and forth in a cubical box of side-length L with velocities v, one-third in the east-west direction, one-third in the north-south direction, and one-third in the vertical direction, with momentum changes in each perpendicular elastic collision with a wall of Mv to –Mv every 2L/v seconds.

What would the pressure P be if, by definition, pressure is force F per unit area A, with force equal, according to Newton, to the time rate of change of momentum?

$$P = F(\text{east-west direction})/A = [\Delta(\text{momentum in east-west direction})/\Delta t]/A$$

$$= [(Mv) - (-Mv) \times n/3] / [2L/v] / L^2$$

$$= (1/3) \, n \, M \, v^2 / L^3$$

$$= (1/3\} \, m \, v^2/ V$$

$$= (2/3) \, [(1/2)mv^2] / V$$

$$= (2/3) \, \{\text{translational kinetic energy, KE}] / V$$

$$= (2/3) \, [\text{KE density}]$$

Molecular velocity v occurs in the expression $P = (2/3) \, m \, v^2 / V$ *squared:* once as a measure of the *intensity* of molecule-wall collisions; and once as a measure of the *frequency* of such collisions.

Physical Significance of the Temperature T

Throughout the program on "Flames and Explosions" it was supposed that *random molecular velocities increase with increasing temperature.* A simple argument supports that important supposition. To see it set equal to each other expressions for pressure P for ideal gases from the Gas Laws and from (above) Kinetic Molecular Theory.

$$P = nRT/V = (1/3)nMv^2/V \rightarrow RT = (1/3)Mv^2$$
or
$$(1/2)Mv^2 \, [= \text{ Molar Kinetic Energy of Translational Motion}] = (3/2)RT$$

The corresponding molar heat capacity at constant volume, C_v, is given by the expression:

$$C_V = (3/2)R(T_2 - T_1)/(T_2 - T_1) = (3/2)R$$

$$= (3/2)(1.9873 \text{ cal/K mole}) = 2.9810 \text{ cal/K mole.}$$

That is exactly the molar heat capacity at constant volume of the noble gases (R/2 for each translational degree of freedom).

The Periodic System

First-row elements in the 6-colum block of periodic tables, such as oxygen, are highly distinctive compared to other members of their Groups. Compare, e.g., oxygen with sulfur and sulfur with selenium and tellurium. Both, like sulfur, and unlike oxygen, are solid, single-bonded elements.

Especially distinctive are first-row elements in the 2-column block, if one locates in that block hydrogen, an s^1 system, above lithium, another s^1 system, and helium, an s^2 system, above beryllium, another s^2 system. Both locations satisfy the Rule of First-Element Distinctiveness, in spades!, and the Triad Rule.

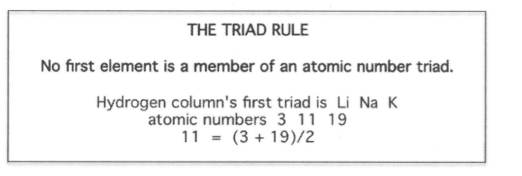

THE TRIAD RULE

No first element is a member of an atomic number triad.

Hydrogen column's first triad is Li Na K
atomic numbers 3 11 19
$11 = (3 + 19)/2$

First-element distinctiveness is less pronounced in the 10-column block, all of whose elements are metals.

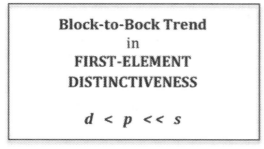

Block-to-Bock Trend
in
FIRST-ELEMENT
DISTINCTIVENESS

$$d < p << s$$

The term "block" refers to the shapes of periodic tables, easily captured in the following fashion.

Directions for Capturing the Periodic Table
Using Dobereiner's First Triad and Atomic Numbers

List horizontally equally spaced elements' atomic numbers 1 through 120. Put in bold face, and, for further emphasis, underline, atomic numbers for Dobereiner's first triad Ca Sr Ba [atomic numbers 20 38 56, with 38 (the triad's middle member) $= (20 + 56)/2$]. Do likewise for atomic numbers 4 (Be), 12 (Mg), 88 (Rn), and 120; they are other members of the Ca-Sr-Ba group. Illustrated is Mendeleev's statement of the Periodic Law, if one substitutes atomic numbers for his "atomic weighs".

```
1  2  3  4  5  6  7  8  9  10  11  12  13  14  15  16  17  18  19  20  21  22  23  24  25
26  27  28  29  30  31  32  33  34  35  36  37  38  39  40  41  42  43  44  45  46  47  48  49  50
51  52  53  54  55  56  57  58  59  60  61  62  63  64  65  66.  67  68  69  70  71  72  73  74  75
76  77  78  79  80  81  82  83  84  85  86  87  88  89  90  91  92  93  94  95  96  99  98  99  100
101  102  103  104  105  106  107  108  109  110  111  112  113  114  115  116  117  118  119  120
```

Omit (here at the outset) elements 1 and 2 (whose locations in the Periodic System are controversial).

Break the remaining sequence of atomic numbers (3 – 120) into periods in which highlighted numbers are lined up in a single vertical column, with no gaps within periods or columns. (Gaps meant for Mendeleev missing elements.) *Strive for maximum regularity in lengths of periods and columns.* Produced is the Left Step Form of the Periodic Table, sans H and He.

Locate hydrogen and helium so as to maximize overall regularity, particularly with respect to occurrence of periods in *pairs*, as to their lengths (called "dyads").

H and He complete the first dyad (together with Li and Be , atomic numbers 3 and 4).

If periods are numbered downward, 1 to 8, the order of occupancy of locations in the Left Step form of the Periodic Table with increasing atomic number is given, *without exception*, by the following -

Periodic System Location Rule

Smallest period number first and, for a given period number, widest block first.

In a series of articles in English by Mendeleev regarding his classification of the elements, as *atoms*, according to the Periodic Law (stated in terms of *atomic* weights or *atomic* numbers), Mendeleev discussed what he called "*atom*analogies". A striking atomanalogy is suggested by the shape of the left step form of the periodic table.

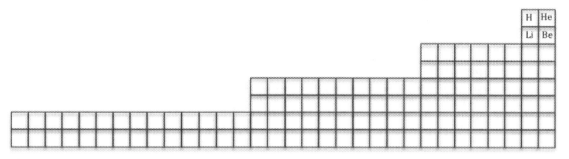

Atomic hydrogen is to atomic lithium, suggests the table, as atomic helium is to atomic beryllium.

$$H : Li :: He : Be$$

Stated algebraically, for a numerical atomanalogy,

$$H/Li = He/Be$$

One of the most of atomic of atomic properties (along with atomic numbers and atomic weights) are atoms' first stage ionization energies. Letting elements' symbols stand for those energies (in eV) yields the expression -

$$H/Li = 13.6/5.6 = \mathbf{2.5} \approx \mathbf{2.6} = 24.6/9.32 = He/Be$$

(For comparison: He/Ne = 24.6/21.6 = 1.14)

To begin periods with elements whose maximum oxidation numbers are +1, move the 2-column block on the far right to the far left.

To diminish the table's width, footnote elements of the 14-column block.

To further shorten the table, footnote the 10-column block, rendering the 14-column footnote a footnote to a footnote.

Except for the 2-column block, blocks begin with elements whose maximum oxidation numbers are +3 (B & Al, Sc & Y, La & Ac), because outer s-block electrons are oxidizable, valence shell electrons for all elements.

Capturing the Periodic Table in the manner described above is similar in one respect to teaching from demonstration-experiments and in using valence sphere models of molecular electron density profiles. Sidestepped in the three instances is a need to use atomic orbitals. Avoided, accordingly, are mathematical difficulties associated with Schrödinger's equation, the only source of such orbitals.

Statements of Electronic Spatial Exclusion

The Noncrossing Rule
Valence strokes of classical bond diagrams never cross each other.

Lewis's Induction
Valence strokes represent two electrons.

Implications of the Noncrossing Rule and Lewis's Induction
Two but no more than two electrons can be at the same region of space at the same time.

Also: the 2-electron systems H_2 and He have *finite molar volumes*.
Two electrons can be at the same region of space at the same time, but not two electron pairs.

Related Statements by Two Nobel Laureates in Physics

BORN: *The probability of a system's electronic configuration is proportional to the square of the configuration's wave function:* $\Psi^2(1, 2, \ldots)$.

"1" and "2" stand for space and spin coordinates of electrons 1 and 2.

HEISENBERG: *Electrons are indistinguishable.* If we switch labels for electrons 1 and 2, then, according to Born, -

$$\Psi^2(1, 2, \ldots) = \Psi^2(2, 1, \ldots)$$

Take the square root.

$$\Psi(1, 2, \ldots) = \pm \Psi(2, 1, \ldots)$$

Choose the minus sign.

$$\Psi(1, 2, \ldots) = -\Psi(2, 1, \ldots)$$

For suppose, then, that electrons 1 and 2 have the same spin and are at the same place at the same time. Then coordinate "1" = coordinate "2", say X, yielding -

$$\Psi(X, X, \ldots) = -\Psi(X, X, \ldots)$$
$$\longrightarrow$$
$$\Psi(X, X, \ldots) = 0$$
$$\longrightarrow$$
$$\Psi^2(X, X, \ldots) = 0$$

*The probability that two spin-parallel electrons
are at the <u>same point</u> at the same time is zero.*

"Same point" is, admittedly, not the same thing as the "same region of space". But it's a step in that direction.

The Born/Heisenberg statement of exclusion from physics does not contradict the Lewis/classical-theory statement of exclusion from chemistry, nor does the latter statement contradict the former statement. Each statement lends credence to the other statement.

Electronic Structure of an Active Metal

In visualizing a mechanism for the reaction of a Bronsted acid (a proton donor) with an active metal (an electron donor), yielding a doubly protonated electron pair (a molecule of dihydrogen), it helps to have a mental image of a model of the electronic structure of an active metal. One route to such a model begins with –

The Isoelectronic Principle

Molecules that have the same number of atomic cores, other than H^+, and the same number of valence electrons often have similar arrangements of atomic cores and electron domains.

Protonation and deprotonation of an electron domain little alters the overall shape of an electron cloud.

Molecules of methane, ammonia, and water have essentially the same bond angles.

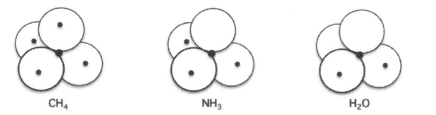

Similarly, alchemical proton transfers of the protons of the hydride ions (H^-) of potassium hydride (K^+H^-) transform a valence sphere model of potassium hydride into a valence sphere model of "calcium electride", $Ca^{+2}(e_2^{-2})$.

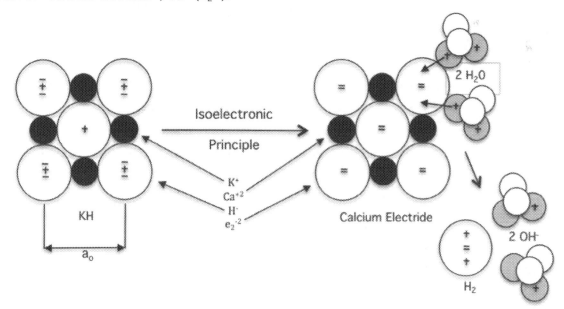

Shown at the right is protonation of an exposed electride ion of calcium electride, isoelectronic with potassium hydride, by two water molecules yielding a dihydrogen molecule and two hydroxide ions of two deprotonated water molecules.

$$e_2^{-2} + 2\ H_2O(l) = 2\ OH^-(aq) + H_2(g)$$

followed by
$$2\ OH^-(aq) + Ca^{+2}(aq) = Ca(OH)_2(c) + Heat!$$

PRINCIPLES OF IMPOTENCE
The First and Second Laws of Thermodynamics

We can't win.

Impossible is any event whose sole effect is a change in the –

- elevation of a body
- velocity of a body
- temperature of a body
- chemical composition of a body

The Energy of the Universe is conserved.

$$\Delta E(universe) = 0$$

Energy cannot be created or destroyed, only transformed.

Conserve energy? We can't help but do so!
What's meant: Conserve *transformable* forms of energy.

For a universe of discourse = a system + the system's thermal and mechanical surroundings:

$$\Delta E(universe) = \Delta E(system) + \Delta E(thermal\ surroundings) + \Delta E(mechanical\ surroundings) = 0$$
$$\rightarrow$$
$$\Delta E(sys) = -\Delta E(th\ surr) - \Delta E(mech\ surr) = \text{"Q"} + \text{"W"}$$

$Q = -\Delta E(th\ surr)$ = energy lost by the thermal surroundings of a system to the system
$W = -\Delta E(mech\ surr)$ = energy lost by the mechanical surroundings of a system to the system

We can't even break even.

Impossible is any event whose sole effect is the exact opposite of -

- friction: transformation of mechanical energy to heat (KELVIN)
- expansion of a gas into a region of lower pressure (PLANCK)
- heat flow from a low to a higher temperature (CLAUSIUS)
- any natural, spontaneous event (MOVIES REVERSED LOOK ODD)

The Entropy of the Universe tends to increase.

It cannot be destroyed, only created,
or left unchanged, in reversible events.

$$\Delta S(universe) \geq 0$$
$$\Delta_{rev}S(universe) = 0$$

$$\Delta S(mech\ surr) = 0$$
[Purely mechanical events are reversible.]
$$\rightarrow$$
$$\Delta S(univ) = \Delta S(sys) + \Delta S(th\ surr)$$
$$\rightarrow$$
$$\Delta S(sys) = -\Delta S(th\ surr) + \Delta S(univ)$$
$$\rightarrow$$
$$\Delta S(sys) = -\Delta_{rev}S(th\ surr)$$

$$\Delta S(th\ surr) = \Delta E(th\ surr)/T$$
[by definition $T = \Delta E(th\ surr)/\Delta S(th\ surr)$]
$$\rightarrow$$
$$\Delta S(sys) = -\Delta_{rev}E(th\ surr)/T = Q_{rev}/T = 0$$

Every demonstration-experiment illustrates the 1st and 2nd Laws of Thermodynamics.

A Handout for Programs on Flames and Explosions

A Summary of the Conceptual Side of the Fundamental Antithesis of Science Between Things and Thoughts, Nature and Man Added to Nature
through

A FOCUS ON FUNDAMENTALS

"It was amazing how closely the program [a Van Visit] tied in with what we're currently studying."
SEVENTH GRADE TEACHER

Because fundamentals apply to many situations, programs that feature fundamentals
tie in with many aspects of school curricula.

Atoms: What every thing is made of. Conserved in ordinary events. Thus, what goes in must come out or pile up. Hence, the possibility of recycling, pollution, and obesity.

Gases: Chiefly empty space. Huge increases in volume occur when solids and liquids gasify (endothermically). The physical basis of steam technology for harnessing the power of fire.

Collision Theory: To react chemically in name-changing changes of matter (e.g.: "Hydrogen" + "Oxygen" = "Water"), molecules must collide with each other physically with bond-breaking violence. Hence cooks' imperative: Mix and Heat. And firemen's Triangle of Fire: Fuel + Oxidizer + Activation (all at the same place at the same time) = Fire.

Wastes: Do not support events that produce them. Nothing can live on its own wastes. Thus use of the oxides of carbon ("carbon dioxide") and hydrogen ("dihydrogen oxide") to extinguish ordinary fires (of fuels composed of C, H, and O atoms).

Atomic and Molecular Disorder: Tends to increase. Never, over all, decreases. The Universe never passes through the same state twice. Nature makes no U-turns. Time marches onward. Things age. They never "youth". We can't go back, in every respect. All events, all things considered, are irreversible, says the Second Law of Thermodynamics.

1st and 2nd Laws of Thermodynamics: Energy is conserved. Entropy tends to increase.

The Entropy Ethic: Minimize your footprint on the environment. Live leanly. Do not create entropy — a numerical measure of atomic and molecular disorder — unnecessarily. Conserve transformable forms of energy. Remember: Power is the haste with which energy is transformed, usually to heat. Haste makes waste, thermal pollution, and entropy.

Kinetic-Molecular Theory: $P(\text{Ideal Gas}) = (1/3) nMv^2/V$.

Gas Laws of Boyle, Charles, and Avogadro: Summarized by the expression $P = nRT/V$.

Absolute Temperature T: Proportional (according to the previous two statements) to the translational kinetic energy of the molecules of an ideal gas. The higher T, the larger molecules' kinetic energies, $(1/2)mv^2$.

The Phase Rule: $F = C - P + 2$. A single phase ($P = 1$) of a pure substance ($C = 1$) has 2 degrees of freedom: say T and P. If present as 3 phases, it has 0 degrees of freedom.

The Periodic Law: The chemical elements, if arranged according to their atomic numbers, exhibit an evident periodicity of properties.

The Principle of Spatial Exclusion of Electrons: Suggested by the fact that liquid dihydrogen has a finite molar volume, however great the pressure, and by Lewis's induction that valence strokes, which never cross each other, represent two electrons. Evidently two electrons can occupy the same region of space at the same time, but not three.

Faraday's Reasons for His Focus on "First Principles" in His Public Lectures on Chemistry

"On considering at the commencement of the course what ought to be the nature of these lectures [on chemistry at the Royal Institution for the general public; and, one might add, of Van Visits to schools], they appeared to me to admit of two distinct characters: they might be illustrative of the various processes and applications in the arts which are of a chemical character; or they might be elementary in their nature, and explanatory of the *secret laws and forces* on which the science of chemistry, with all its uses, is founded.

"These two modes in which chemistry may be said to exist form the extremes of our knowledge on the subject; the first or applicative ['applied'] chemistry, is identical with the knowledge and practice of the artisan and manufacturer, and is also that from which we gain our first perception and idea [about chemistry]; the second, or elementary ['pure'] chemistry, is the result of our researches *in the science,* and though, being the result of long and laborious trains of inductive reasoning and experimental investigation, it is the last production of the mind, yet it is the basis upon which nature and art [man added to nature] have raised practical science [to a subject worthy of inclusion in schools' curricula].

"To have made these lectures, therefore, illustrative of the arts and manufacturers, would have been to repeat what the man of observation had already noticed, i.e. the results of general experience."

'Applicative chemistry' (the chemistry of 'general experience') is familiar chemistry. 'The last production of the mind' (pure chemistry: man added to nature) is, even for 'the acute man', generally unfamiliar chemistry.

"The acute man may observe very accurately, but it does not follow that he should reason perfectly or extensively. To tell a person that a stone falls to the ground would be to insult him, but it would not at all compromise his character for sagacity to be informed of the laws by which the stone descends [and, ultimately] remains at rest.

"I know of no illustration of the arts and manufacturers of the civilized world, which would have been worth my offering, or your acceptance, not founded on *first principles* [listed in the previous appendix]."

Faraday is saying that he will explain what is shown and described. Of course, young students may not understand everything, or even very much, of what a scientist says about demonstration-experiments, beyond, perhaps, names for things and events, which, however, they love to use, and which, in fact, are first steps toward fuller comprehension. They may understand, moreover, intuitively, that there's something being said that someday they may be able to understand more fully. Hence, perhaps, their frequent efforts to witness the same program repeatedly, by skipping such activities as recess and lunch.

Audience Responses to Teaching from Demonstration-Experiments
in
Van Visits to Schools

Reproduced on the following pages are selections from thank you notes received from students and teachers, principles and parents thrilled by Van Visits to their schools.

Teachers were asked to have their students tell their visitors which demos they liked best. Demos seldom cited were dropped from programs, which, in time, came to consist solely of demos "liked best".

Students' Comments

"Fun!" "Cool!" "Neat!" "Splendid!" "Excellent!" "Exhilarating!" "Fabulous!" "Fantastic!" "Action-filled. Great!" "Terrific!" "Spectacular!" "Awesome!" "Outstanding!" "Exciting!" "Fascinating!" "Surprising!" "Suspenseful!" "Thrilling!" "Stimulating!" "Inspiring!"

"Action-filled." "Interesting." "Amusing." "Intriguing." "Entertaining." "Educational." "Informative." "Well-set up." "Organized." "Smoothly run." "Clear." "Easily followed." "Understandable."

"It was good to know that people in the science world care about us and what we are learning." "Thanks for the GREAT show." "It's the best assembly yet." "The best thing this year." "Much better than Mr. Wizard." "It was better than the circus." "I loved it."

"I loved the chemistry." "The science class was the most fun class we've ever had." "I haven't enjoyed science more in my life." "I couldn't believe some of the things you did." "All of my classmates were amazed by all the experiments you presented us."

"Everything was so great I can't choose what I liked best." "I liked all of the things you did." "I don't think you should change anything." "I wish the program could have been longer than an hour." "I never knew chemistry could be so much fun."

"I never knew science could be so much fun." "I never knew chemistry could be so fascinating." "You taught me that science can be fun." "You showed me a whole new way of looking at science." "The only thing I didn't like was that it was too short. If it had lasted all day it would be a lot better."

"Your job looks pretty neat to me." "You guys looked like you enjoyed your work." "I hope when I grow up I can do what you do." "Yesterday's class was so much fun, I want to be a chemist." "We [two young girls] want you to know that here and now we have decided to become chemists." "It inspired me to be a chemist." "It sparked interest in chemistry in many."

"You changed my mind: someday I might want to be a chemist." "I'm really thinking about becoming a chemist because of your assembly." "You have encouraged me to take science more carefully." "You should realize that you have recruited many students to enter your field." "Now when I go to science class I cannot wait." "I am looking forward to starting chemistry class next year."

"The people who haven't had chemistry yet will have a head start and the ones who have it now I think understand it more." "Everyone learned a great deal and an interest in chemistry either remarkably sprouted up or was rekindled." "Dr. Bent's program is something I will never forget."

"I learned all sorts of things from your presentation." "You can do a lot of stuff with science I learned." "You taught a lot about gases and fire." "You taught me a lot about gases and safety." "I learned a lot about explosions." "You showed me that when gases are mixed together you can do a lot of things."

"Not only did you teach us about gases, you showed us how everything works." "I didn't know all those gases were real." "I learned about the triangle of fire." "Before I came I knew what a cold front was but you made it a lot more clear to me by actually showing me what happens."

"I never knew there could be a liquid at –196 $^{\circ}$C." "It was good for those who don't know what mother nature's chemicals can do." "At first I didn't believe a word you were saying about the candle, but when you think about it, it's the truth, plain and simple."

"When I got home I told my parents about the whole program." "I was so excited when I got home I told my parents about it." "I told my grandfather what we learned and he said he would have liked to have seen it too."

"You really got kids involved." "I really enjoyed your 'hands on' experiments." "I was the volunteer, the girl with glasses." "I had a great time helping with the program." "It was really neat to be able to touch the 'dry ice'." "My favorite was when we drank carbon dioxide."

"I felt the heat when the balloon exploded." "I tried the experiment with the balloon and the pan at home. It worked!"

"Thank you for all the time and skills you gave us." "Thank you for sharing your knowledge with us." "You really knew what you were talking about." "Please write." "I wish we could see you again." "Please come back." "I hope you'll keep doing this so other schools can see it too."

Teachers' Comments

"That was the most educational assembly we ever had. Students were unanimously excited and full of comments and questions throughout the day."

"In the words of our students, 'This was the best assembly we've eve3r had.'"

"Thank you so very much for presenting the best program ever to the students and staff of Wellsburgh Middle school. We were all so impressed with the entire day. Your program was spectacular and it made National Education Week a big hit in our school. Please keep us in mind for any new programs."

"It was one of the best age appropriate and entertaining assemblies that we have ever scheduled."

"Many students have said that it was the best assembly that we've ever had. In fact, the principal told me that he has gotten phone calls from parents congratulating him for the assembly based solely on the excitement that their children brought home that day. For my part, I am delighted to have this frame of reference to use in my chemistry classes."

"All students and teachers were treated to an exciting, entertaining, and informative evening of Chemistry. The demonstrations were all the students wanted to talk about for the entire week."

"The Chemistry Van Program at Pitt is a great motivational tool. The people involved in this program do a fantastic job. Pitt is to be commended for its support of this program."

"Your show was magnificent and your mini-sessions were just as exciting! Your obvious love and enthusiasm for what you are doing made your program exceptional."

"I was totally captivated by the entire presentation — the rockets (outside) were especially fun! The boys thought they were 'awesome.'"

"I loved the way you made the kids THINK. No lectures—yea! Your demonstrations were out of sight—all right! If there is one thing my kids love to do it is to think. Thank you for providing them with this marvelous opportunity. Well done!"

"All I can say with my social science background is 'WOW!' I was impressed with your demonstrations. Will you please come back again? It's really hard to get a reaction from 8th graders, but you did it again and again and again."

"In this day and age of TV, VCRs, and movies, how does a teacher capture the imagination of a student—especially at the junior high level? Well, if she's smart, she invites Dr. Warnock to her school! My students are hooked on chemistry. Thanks so much."

"I can honestly say that Drs. Garry Warnock and Dave D'Emilio turned our students on to science. Their low key style, as well as their stunning science 'tricks', had our students on the edge of their seats for the entire ninety minute presentation."

"What a great learning experience you shared with us! The students are still talking about your visit. As their science teacher, I'm delighted that you filled them with enthusiasm for science. Your demonstrations were not just flashy but also informative. They were right on target with many things our junior high pupils have been learning. We look forward to your return."

"Thanks again for the wonderful chemistry lesson you gave our fifth graders yesterday. Your demonstrations went far beyond what I would have been able to teach about gases, both in the materials you used and the concepts you presented. I learned a lot from you, too."

"The Van Program has so far reached more than nine hundred students at Knoxville Middle School, some of whom are now in high school college bound programs. I am always astounded by the interest shown by my students in the visiting classroom and assembly programs and how this interest is carried through the entire year and beyond."

"Your program was exactly what our students need and we can't give them."

Principals' Comments

"On Monday, May 11, 1992, our children experienced what may have been their most exciting academic experience of their lives. Your Van Program had the entire school motivated. As a former science teacher and administrator for 35 years, I have never seen students and teachers so enthusiastic about a program."

"The Chemistry Van is the best presentation of scientific information that I have seen from the standpoint of scholarship, student involvement, and the inquiry method."

"Certainly your program was full of many interesting facts (and sounds), but more than anything it was filled with the love you both have for what you are doing and that is probably the greatest lesson for today's children to learn."

"The next day, parents told me 'Mr. Science' [their term, not ours] was the topic of the dinner table conversation. You couldn't keep the children quiet. They talked non-stop about what they had seen."

"The following day I had telephone calls from parents asking us about the program and telling me for the first time that their child came home expressing such excitement about a science lesson."

"I must share with you the reaction of many parents to this program. Parents commented on the interest in chemistry generated and how it affirmed a desire to study chemistry further."

"Everyone is still talking about the program and how wonderful it was. Parents ask me how much we paid for the program and it was nice to tell them it was free. Your enthusiasm for science impressed all the teachers, too. The most frequent question I get asked when your name comes up is, 'When is he coming back?'"

"One of my teachers attended the E-Cube '91 Teacher Workshop at IUP, and she hasn't been the same since! She's been stirring up a storm by telling everyone about your exciting chemistry demonstrations."

"The Van Program is an excellent supplement to our science curriculum and gave our students an added dimension that teachers are not able to provide."

"Due to the outstanding motivation and interest created by the program, I have requested a continued interactive relationship with the 'Science Van' and its personnel for the future."

Parents' Comments

"From what I've heard, I really missed a fantastic performance at Resurrection School! My own children couldn't stop talking about it. We are all looking forward to Part II, scheduled for Feb. 5th."

"Many students felt this assembly to be one of the best witnessed here at St. Germaine School. Our staff of teachers was equally impressed and praised your program. Congratulations to the University or Pittsburgh for acknowledging and providing the Van Program."

"I have heard nothing but 'rave reviews' from the staff, and the kids were in awe. Enclosed are the photos we took. Mr. Hecker plans to be in touch regarding follow-up classroom programs. Again, thank for your interest in teaching science to all children!"

"Thank you very much for coming to our School Support Group Meeting. I've heard nothing but raves from the children and their parents. I was amazed at all the things you brought and

<u>everything you were able to demonstrate for the kids</u>. Who knows but that there were future scientists in that group of children who watch you so intently and with such wonder!"

"We really appreciated all of your time that you gave us with your program. The students in grades 4, 5, & 6 couldn't get enough. You were the 'talk' of the school for days. The kids even went home and talked it up with their parents. They must have been impressed. The students in grades K through 3 thought you were truly magical. All 870 students and their teachers would like to say thank you again."

"Being responsible for PTA programming at the elementary and middle school levels, I truly have come to appreciate school programs that are both entertaining and educational. Those types of programs are scarce and a delight to find. The 'Pitt Chemistry Van' is certainly one of those programs."

"The students responded to Dr. Warnock's and Mr. D'Emilio's 'theatrical' demonstration of the properties of gases with enthusiasm and interest. The teaching staff was notably impressed by their skillful presentation as well as their open and approachable manner. My own son, who is looking toward a career in science, was thrilled to prove (to some kids who tease him) that scientists <u>aren't</u> 'nerds' and that science really can be fun. I have received so much positive feedback that I was compelled to write to urge support of this program in the future."

"My son came home so excited about science, I just want to say thank you, with the enclosed check. I hope you keep up your splendid work."

Local Media's Comments

Fireballs and explosions rocked the Apollo-Ridge High School auditorium last Wednesday morning. Not to worry though, it was all part of the big show put on by the University of Pittsburgh Science Outreach Program in the hope of turning on the middle school student body to the fun of science.

Wizards Dave D'Emilio, director of the Center for Chemistry Demonstrations, and Dr. Gary Warnock, an associate in the department, presented "Triangles of Fire and Life", a traveling laboratory about the chemistry and physics of combustion.

The program, originally designed by Dr. Henry, has been in operation for the last two and one half years.

The purpose is to bring to schools the type of experiments not likely to be seen in the ordinary school lab. Schools in the Tri-State area from kindergarten to college are visited by the entertaining team of scientists.

On this particular occasion, the reactions were extraordinary, both on the stage, as in chemical reactions, and in the audience, as in "oohs, ahs, and wows".

One "attention getter" after another entertained the crowd.

The show ran from fire bursts of helium [!], hydrogen, methane and propane to cannons and pop bottle rockets. It then proceeded from pitchers of invisible CO_2 gas, incidentally, consumed by one of the students and described as tasting like soda pop, to cloud-making and explosions.

In the midst of all the fun and games, learning received the attention it deserves and most everyone came away with a lessened fear of science.

Larry Cignetti, who invited the group to Apollo-Ridge, could not have been more satisfied with the responses.

"It makes science more interesting and understandable. It upgrades the process of educating students to science," said Cignetti. "We need more of this type of program."

"It was amazing how closely the program tied in with what we're currently studying," said a seventh grade teacher.*

All in all it could be said that the University of Pittsburgh has found the right formula for success in science education. The Apollo-Ridge Middle School would agree.

EXCERPS FROM STAFF REPORTS ON VAN VISITS

STAFF: HB Director. GW Assistant Director. JB High School Chemistry Teacher on Sabbatical Leave. CB & MS Chemistry Graduate Students.

Workshop for Elementary School Teachers, GW. I began by showing slides of Van Visits. I'd planned to do that for less than three minutes, but the audience was highly amused by the slides and commentary. Teachers gave me a standing ovation. One senior male teacher said "This was the only two hours in the entire two-day conference worth attending." I was astonished by the popularity of the magnetic modules [for constructing bond diagrams]. "They're so simple!" said the teachers. "And so inexpensive!" My conclusions: <u>The outreach program is the only way to do research in education</u>. MAGNETIC MODULES ARE GOOD.

Yeshiva School, GW. The demos soon drew an adjacent class out of their room. It was clear that students had never seen presentations like mine.

Greenwald Elementary School, HB. "It was the finest program we've ever had," the head science teacher said. Another teacher said, "You did a good job at getting down to their level." One student wondered about something about a balloon inflated with a flammable gas and torched that we had never discussed. "How did you put it out?" It's a marvelous question to put to an audience.

Freeport Junior High School, HB. A program of demonstration-experiments with a teammate offers opportunities to exhibit team work. "You fellows really had your act together," remarked a teacher. [On another visit a teacher asked, "How many years have you two been working together?" Actually, for only a few Van Visits.]

West Virginia Wesleyan College, Chemistry Scholarship Breakfast for Alumni, HB. Breakfasters, ages 8 – 88, worked their way through activities described in a handout "Playing with a Candle." Afterwards several alumni told their host that the guest's talk about "The Appeal of Authentic Science" was the best talk they'd ever heard. He'd allowed Nature to do most of the "talking".

Workshop for Elementary School Teachers, JB. The director of the workshop asked me to go beyond the allotted time, "by popular demand". I was surprised to learn that 80 percent of the elementary school teachers are either incompetent or uncomfortable with science instruction. Their students emerge thinking that "science is a dumb subject" [which it's been: in large part meaningless vocabulary drill].

St. Alexander Elementary School, HB. At the outset students wanted each demo done again. A good way to introduce demos to young students is to ask, "Would you like to see . . .?" They always say "YES!"

Peters Township High School, HB. Chemistry "learned" from books may be profoundly misleading. Students were amazed to see soap bubbles blown with hydrogen and with mixtures of hydrogen and oxygen, for they had "learned" that hydrogen is "explosive". They didn't really believe, at first, that we had real hydrogen in our balloons.

Knoxville Middle School, MS. On seeing liquid nitrogen boil, a number of students wondered, "Is it hot?" Interesting and instructive to see at this point is ice-water at water's triple point boiling.

St. Albert the Great, HB. This was a great visit. We were very close to the audience. Student's attention span seem unlimited. We went on for three hours. Afterwards the Principal said, "There was much more to program than chemistry."

Trafford Elementary and Middle Schools, HB. Students, teachers, and administrators were "sky high" after the visit. "That's exactly what our students and teachers need," said the Principle. His chief question: "Does the university have other programs like that?"

Westmoreland Community College, GW. Adults enjoyed the demos even more than did the kids. [Every fact that one knows is a potential hook on which to hang new ideas.]

McCreary School, JB. Students were asked how one might improve the performance of the bottle rocket. Most of them thought that it needed more fuel [easily checked with a simple experiment.] None suggested changing its temperature [another simple thing to do]. [Almost any demo, fully investigated, can occupy a full class period. A companion to that remark is Gil Haight's remark: "I illustrate all of chemistry with hydrogen plus oxygen."]

Valley Christian Academy, MS. Would it be all right to have a few explosions for the K – 1 group? we wondered. "No problem," said a teacher. Most of the children's fathers are avid hunters. Their kids are used to loud noises. She was right. They loved the loud noises.

Central Elementary School, MS. The kids were extremely enthusiastic. The program lasted for two hours. The new crystal-clear balloons were extremely effective.

Seton-LaSalle High School, HB. A team of four chemists was kept busy doing demos throughout the day. Garry estimated that we did more demos than students normally see in an entire year of a science course — perhaps two science courses. One science teacher said that he especially liked the large number of concepts covered.

Mt. Lebanon High School, HB. The opening assembly was video-taped for later use on local TV. "What's your favorite demo?" asked a student in a post-assembly session. Told that our answer would be essentially the same as the conductor Pierre Monteau's answer to the question "What's your favorite music?", he guessed correctly: It's the demo you're doing now.

West Mifflin Middle School, CB. Some students had seen a Van Program last year, but there was no lack of interest or enthusiasm. [A demo worth doing is worth doing more than once.] <u>The best group of students was the group with the worst reputation for behavior</u>. [Rambunctious youths are like eager scientists. They like to do things and see what happens. Teachers constantly saying "Sit down!" "Be quiet!" cause schools to filter out and discard potential scientists.]

Horace Mann Elementary School, GW. The principle, much taken by our program, asked for detailed descriptions of the experiments and wondered if he could write letters on our behalf.

West Hills Elementary School, JB. Classroom activities were directed primarily by student questions. Ten students skipped lunch so that they could work with dry ice and see it liquefied in clamped tygon tubing. One parent, present at the assembly, said that it was "better than going to the Carnegie Science Center."

Brooke High School, West Virginia, GW. Main lesson: Set off with LOTS if time to spare. The trip was one of the most enjoyable for me. The success formula was simply this: lots of time to do things properly. A teacher said that it was the best program they had ever had at the school, even better than one they had last year that was still being talked about.

St. Regis School, JB. One of the cafeteria ladies told me the students at lunch were so excited about the program she had to stay and watch. Many students came around afterwards to try the "dry pop" activity,

Whitehall Elementary School, HB. Young audiences LOVE to volunteer their teachers to be atoms in skits of kinetic-molecular models of chemical reactions.

Fort Allen Elementary School, JB. Each 30 minute assembly follow-up session ended with about eight to ten students disappointed because we didn't get to their second or third questions.

Monesson Middle School, JB. Student interest and involvement was high in all classes. A teacher commented, however, that her "best classes" were the most reluctant to get involved and that some of her "lower level classes" exhibited the most enthusiasm and came through with the best answers. [Schools are turning learning on its head. The creative and disruptive are the "lower level". The obedient and nondisruptive are the "best".]

North American Martyrs School, MS. The students were excited, informed, and cooperative. We never got to all their questions in post-assembly sessions. So many of the 4th-6th graders stayed around after they were dismissed that the teachers had to chase them to their buses. Parents providing rides had to come in to get their children.

Central Elementary School, HB. The distinctive feature of this visit was extensive, highly popular use of student volunteers. "Regulars" were trained at the outset during set-up time. They were then used to select and instruct volunteers during programs. It seemed that every student in the school wanted to be a volunteer. Students asked excellent questions that led to interesting demonstrations.

Cleveland ACS Section Awards Night, HB. All members of the audience seemed to thoroughly enjoy executing Faraday's experiments with a candle. Scientists from NASA's Lewis Research Center reported that burning candles in a tall micro-gravity facility burned for at least 5 seconds, which means that extinction of our candles in the falling flask demo must arise from "blow off". NASA has candle experiments planned for a satellite (as I had suggested some years ago).

SSP Saturday "Focus on Spectroscopy", Buhl Science Center, HB. Students who had seen van programs before seemed to be the most interested ones. They sat up front, volunteered to help with the demos, and were the first ones to offer answers to our questions. They seemed to remember *everything* that they'd seen and heard before. Everyone seemed disappointed when we had to stop after two hours. The octane cannon, shot off outdoors, set of several car alarms a block or so away, much to everyone's amusement.

George Washington Carver School of Engineering and Science, Philadelphia, PA, HB. The students were super-assistants. On request of one of the teachers we exploded two pop bottles partially filled with liquid nitrogen, and then capped, in a large parking lot after school before the entire student body. The local police had been informed and were present in force. Nature did her thing, impressively, shattering, along with the bottles, a warm-water-filled plastic dish pan in which one bottle had been placed. Again, several car alarms were set off.

All Schools. Each van visit is an adventure. All visits have been successful. Some 98 percent have been *highly* successful. Only three of 138 visits during one school year were, relatively speaking, disappointments, to the staff. Even those visits, however, were judged by the majority of the people in the audiences to have been *excellent* visits. The most often asked question has been: "When can you come back?"

AN EXTRAPOLATION: Every school in the country, kindergarten through twelfth grade, but possibly most especially middle schools, would love to have "Van Visits" by enthusiastic college and university scientists and their students executing safely, describing aptly, and explaining correctly in terms of a kinetic-molecular model of matter striking demonstration-experiments. Estimated cost per sparked student: less than $5.

"How Do You Hold an Audience's Rapt Attention for Several Hours?"

PROFESSOR FRED TABBUTT

Capitalize on the fact that chemistry is the most demonstrable science. Do many simple, short, safe, striking, and surprising demonstration-experiments. Maintain a brisk pace. But do not rush. Provide audiences time for members to compare impressions with each other. Aim to educate, entertain, and to spark enthusiasm for science, in sparkable youths. Drop demos that are not considered by some students to be their favorite demos. Feature—as does Hollywood, in its action movies—flames and explosions. Liquid nitrogen and dry ice are also nice. Keep in mind that many youths feel that bigger is better. Feature phenomena that are easily seen. Seek experiments that have counter-intuitive results (in looking dangerous, but that really aren't). Shun use of "black boxes" between phenomena and viewers. KISS: Keep it Simple Sir. Best results are obtained with the simplest apparatus. Present experiments in a sequence that tells a story. Work on transitions. Design each experiment to follow in some way from the previous one and to lead logically to the next one. Keep introductory remarks—indeed, all remarks—short. Let Nature be a program's star. Launch into the first experiment ASAP. Exhibit teamwork. Show more than chemistry. Exhibit one's love of chemistry. Be enthusiastic and energetic. Use Van Visits to exhibit deeply held values: cooperation, courtesy, competence, integrity, honesty, dependability, foresight, etc. Be efficient. Have one demo being prepared while another one is in progress. Introduce variety. Alternate experiments with explanations, skits, posters, and other visual aids. Use volunteers (even when not necessary). Encourage clapping and chatter following striking events. Chat at such moments with nearby students. But insist on silence during explanations of experiments. Expect audiences to be polite and attentive. Be certain that they are comfortable. Avoid distractions. Execute programs in schools, churches, public auditoriums, and other "sacred places", locations for serious contemplation. Avoid shopping malls. Scale up demos as much as is wise. Stress safety. Point out that safe passages through life are the product of knowledge, experience, memory, logic, and imagination (in imagining the worst things that might happen and preparing for them). Prepare, prepare, and prepare. Then wing it. Don't use notes. (They cause one to lose eye contact, if only briefly, with audiences.) Avoid use and production of toxic substances. Realize that young students (not concerned in life, yet, with earning a living) are more interested in pure science (that, for instance, a candle's flame, with respect to combustion, is hollow) than they are in applied science (that, e.g., a candle's soot, a.k.a. "carbon black", is used in manufacturing automobile tires). Be specific in your examples (of, e.g., flames and explosions) and general in your conclusions (that, for instance, nothing can live on its own wastes). Stress fundamentals. Point out frequently the fundamental antithesis of science between things and thoughts, evidence and inductions. Show, describe, and explain. Avoid numerical calculations of more than a few simple steps. But use arithmetic, where appropriate. Students like that. Emphasize inductive leaps over multistep deductions. Introduce no term or concept unless there is a need for it based on an observation or an experiment. Use facts aggressively to capture ideas. Stress concept-formation over use of formal theories (which are stated in terms of concepts, which, therefore, are more fundamental than theories). Humanize chemistry. Make it seem like a familiar science, which it is, on the practical side (as every thing is made of atoms, the central subject of the Central Science). Note that the Triangle of Ordinary Fire is, also, chemically speaking, the Triangle of the Inner Fires of Life. Use familiar things (such as balloons, plastic bottles, kitchen pans, air, atmospheric pressure, water, baking soda, alcohol, propane torches, and fire extinguishers) in unfamiliar ways. Make the new familiar and the familiar new. Relate human physiology to the Chemical Imperative of the Fires of Life. Have several themes and story lines that connect demos to each other. Shun unexplained demos. Be philosophical. Use analogies. Connect the harnessing of the power of fire by production, and then condensation, of steam to the industrial revolution and the shape of modern civilization. Relate thermal pollution to power production. Use familiar phrases in creative ways. Point out that the cannon was man(un)kind's first internal combustion engine. Introduce the energy function and the Energy Conservation Principle. Illustrate Nature's Second-Law-like nature and cite the Entropy Ethic. (Live leanly. Do not create entropy unnecessarily. Conserve transformable forms of energy—which is what is meant when we're told to "Conserve energy", which we can't help but do!). Work as close to audiences as possible. Make programs interactive. Ask questions: "What would you like to see?" "Would you like to try . . .?" "What do you suppose might happen if . . .?" Never say, "Now I will show you . . .". Say, rather, "Let's see what happens when . . ." Engage teachers and principals in experiments. Students LOVE to see them participate. Use the full expanse of auditoriums and gymnasiums in execution of demos. (Once a bottle rocket aimed at a basketball backboard from far beyond the three-point arc made a basket. (Pure pandemonium!) Pass things around (balloons containing dry ice, dry ice in paper cups of water, plastic sulfur, pennies acted upon by nitric acid, a tennis ball ejected by an octane cannon). Pour liquid nitrogen down an auditorium's sloping aisle and outside on wet grass. Use skits involving students and teachers to simulate kinetic-molecular models of chemical reactions. Speak of chemicals casually, as one would of familiar friends. Carry on conversations with nature. Discuss plans out loud. Respond imaginatively and enthusiastically to occurrence of unexpected events, as opportunities to exhibit oneself as a scientist finding out first-hand how the world works by experimenting, observing what happens, and using the kinetic-molecular model of matter and imagination to suggest reasons for Nature's behavior. Expedite execution of unplanned experiments by having supplementary equipment readily available. Be flexible. Post an agenda with intriguing titles, but depart from it freely. Generate anticipation. Educate audiences to the point where they can guess, intelligently, what might happen next. Shape programs around audiences' questions and suggestions. Build to climaxes. [Some say programs should end in fire (with bottle rockets and an octane cannon). Others think dry ice is nice (when its cold vapors meet humid air).] Provide students, in summary, with "exactly what they need," said a middle school teacher, and that only scientist can give them: approximations to authentic science. In the process: Be friendly. Make eye contacts. Use first names. Be natural. Relax. Smile. Have fun! One could spend a lifetime perfecting execution of Van Visits to schools.

A Hydrogen-Filled Balloon Inadvertently Popped
by
Hot Combustion Products

Mistakes happen.

A student volunteer, in helping to unload a Van in preparation for a program of demonstration-experiments at his school, inadvertently lost his grip on string attached to a hydrogen-filled balloon. Up it rose to the high ceiling of his schools' auditorium, where it came to rest near a recessed light

Thinking that a draft might waft the balloon into the light well where, from the heat of the light, it might pop, allowing its hydrogen to mix with air with which, over wide limits, it forms an explosive mixture that, exploding, might shatter the light and shower glass, perhaps in large chunks, on people seated beneath it — fearing that scenario, and with insufficient time to arrange for retrieval of the balloon before the beginning of a scheduled assembly, arriving audience members were asked to not sit beneath the light.

Eventually the program arrived at one of its climaxes: its largest flame, created by righting an inverted janitor's G.I. barrel full of natural gas beneath the flame of a propane torch taped to a pole, — and, as it turned out, beneath the hydrogen-filled balloon at the ceiling, which the presenters had forgotten about.

Not to worry.

Rising to the ceiling were hot, noncombustible, fire-extinguishing combustion products: carbon dioxide and water, along with dinitrogen, also an extinguisher of ordinary fires.

What happened?

A little pop. Period. Nothing more. The hydrogen did not burn, so far as one could tell. Certainly it did not cause an explosion. The light bulb remained intact. The audience was impressed.

Presenters were reminded that setting back-fires is a method of fighting prairie fires. (And at the end of the school day they had no hydrogen-filled balloon to retrieve.)

Since gases are chiefly empty space and have, accordingly, little capacity for heat, the hot combustion products did not raise combustibles on the other side of the ceiling, bathed in fresh air, to nearly their autoignition temperatures. Consequently, municipal fire-fighters, invited to the program, had nothing to do.

All in all, it was an *educational experience*, for all observers. Van visits are always, to some degree, adventures, with Nature sometimes presenting presenters, unexpectedly, with new demonstration-experiments, such as, in the present instance, a counter-intuitive non-burning-hydrogen-filled-balloon popped, but not exploded, by hot combustion products. A null result — such as non-ignition by hot combustion products of an extremely flammable gas — may be as interesting as a positive result.

Connections

Atomic theory is one of those short cuts which the human mind often takes to raise itself quickly to a height from which the connections between phenomena can be discerned at a glance. CANNIZZARO

Programs' Themes Express Connections. For programs based on Flammable Gases, Dry Ice, and Liquid Nitrogen they include: names of name-changing changes; changes of state; combustion; safety; collision theory; triangles of fire, life, and chemistry; fire extinction; atoms and molecules; kinetic-molecular theory; atomic and molecular weights; Avogadro's Law; gas densities; the scientific method; and seeing similarities in differences, such as dry ice and liquid nitrogen staying cool by evaporation, fire extinctions by their wastes; and oxidations by dioxygen and oxygen-containing potassium chlorate, ferric oxide, water, and carbon dioxide.

Making connections is the business of the mankind dimension of the Fundamental Antithesis of Science between Nature and Man Added to Nature. It distinguishes programs of demonstration-experiments executed, described, and explained from chemical magic shows. It's *why* Van Programs use scientists and their apprentices, not actors, and *how* such programs tell a story.

Nature doing her things is the silent star, mankind making connections the linguistic side of demonstration-experiments described and explained.

Student Exercises Based on Observation and Classification. LIST: different ways hydrogen was burned; familiar things used in unfamiliar ways; unexpected events; how balloons and soap bubbles were used; ways water was used; safety equipment; how it was shown that carbon dioxide is denser than air; illustrations of the principle that flames cannot live on their wastes; illustrations of collision theory; demonstrations of hydrogen's inertness at room temperature; illustrations of the effect of temperature on rates of chemical reactions; gases less dense than air; gases more dense than air; experiments with a candle; examples of action and reaction; instances of condensation; evidence of atmospheric pressure; things illustrated by the bell jar demo; and reasons for using scientists in the design and execution of Van Programs.

KMT. Kinetic-Molecular Theory has tremendous power for making demonstration-experiments make sense. It explains without calculation: gases' low densities (at normal pressures they are chiefly empty space); their tendency to fill available space (their molecules are in rapid, random motion); their condensation on being cooled (their molecules are somewhat sticky); and why there are three familiar states of matter (molecules ordered and touching, touching but not ordered, and not ordered and not touching).

KMT is an indispensable companion when executing potentially hazardous demonstration-experiments. Its correct use in explaining demonstration-experiments and in responding to audience questions requires a familiarity with the energy and entropy functions of the First Law and Second Laws of Thermodynamics.

Van Apprenticeships should include, ideally, seminars by faculty mentors on *General Chemistry from an Advanced Standpoint.*

PRE-PROGRAM STUDENT ACTIVITIES

A Van Visit is no better than preparations for it at *both ends.*

Copy from a good dictionary definitions of these terms:

Hydrogen   Carbon   Nitrogen   Oxygen   Magnesium   Phosphorus

Water   Dew   Steam   Vapor   Vaporization   Boiling   Condensation

Carbon Dioxide   Dry Ice   Sublimation   Absolute Zero   Kelvin   Celsius

Methane   Propane   Gasoline   Oil   Grease   Wax   Paraffin   Polyethylene

Air   Hydrogen Peroxide   Hydrogen Chloride   Acid   Base   Phenolphthalein

Make posters for use by van scientists
of bond diagrams following these rules:

1 "valence stroke" to the symbol H, 2 to O, 3 to N, and 4 to C
with no dangling strokes

for molecules with these formulas:

H_2 O_2 N_2 H_2O H_2O_2 CO_2 CH_4 C_3H_8 C_2H_5OH $(C_2H_5)_2O$

REVIEW EXERCISES

An experience is not a significant experience until it is a thought-registered experience.

Describe, working individually or in teams, for a van experiment in simple, short, declarative sentences *that follow each other logically* what was used, done, seen, said, drawn, imagined, recalled, concluded, and done next.

Students might be told, prior to a Van Visit, of that pending assignment and encouraged to take notes during the visit. That manual activity is said to consolidate transfer of information from presenters' actions to students' minds.

THE BOTTOM LINE

Science in the service of the liberal arts

Better activities for better education through chemistry

Toward Harder Working Students in Schools

If there's one thing that the United States needs in the long run, it's harder working students in schools, especially in science, technology, engineering, and mathematic. Van Visits address that need –

by presenting striking, often counter-intuitive events
> "Everything you did surprised me." "I never knew science could be so much fun."
> "I couldn't believe some of the things you did." "I didn't know science could be so neat and colorful."
> "I didn't know that all those gases were real." "I didn't think the ball would go so far."
> "I never knew there could be a liquid at -196 that was not frozen."

that catch students' attention
> "It was fantastic." "It was fascinating." "The demonstrations were terrific!"
> "The explosions were really amazing." "Your experiments were awesome." "It was spectacular."

and hold it for sustained periods of time
> "It was two hours but you made it seem like ten minutes." "It was the best class I ever had."
> "I would have stayed there all day!" "The only thing wrong was that it was too short."
> "If it lasted all day it would be a lot better."

while the students are being informed
> "I had fun while learning." "Thank you for an interesting and educational program."
> "It taught me a lot about gases and fire!" "Thanks for the lessons about safety."
> "I learned many things, such as nothing can live on its own wastes."
> "I always wondered what was in fire extinguishers."

by hardworking teams of scientists and student apprentices,
> "You must have to really study to learn how to do that." "I bet it took a lot of time to be able to do that."
> "I couldn't believe all the things you brought."
> "I admire all the hard work and dedication you put into your presentation."

who display enthusiasm for their work
> "You showed us how much fun and enthusiasm is in your job."
> "The greatest thing you showed them was your love of science."
> "Now I can't wait to get to get to my science class."

offer explanations for what has been seen (and heard)
> "Thanks for explaining things." "I learned a lot." "I would like to learn more."
> "Not only did you teach us about gases but you showed us how everything works."
> "You helped me understand the reasons the reactions took place, not just the outcomes."

serve as role models
> "When I grow up I think I'll be a chemist." "It inspired me to be a chemist."
> "I hope to be a scientist when I grow up." "I hope when I grow up that I can do what you do."
> "I'm really thinking of becoming a scientists because of your assembly."
> "You should realize that you have recruited many students to enter your field."
> "I tried the experiment with the balloon and the pan. It worked!"
> "I admire your desire to help kids learn and also let them have fun."
> "You must know a lot." "You are lucky to be a scientist."

and conclude with few suggestions.
> Well, what have we been doing? Finding out first-hand how the world works, by doing something [a concluding demo], seeing what happens [Wow!], and thinking about it [this way]. It's called "science", meaning "to know". It's fun. Sometimes it's useful. Society pays people to do it. They're called "scientists". They work in nice surroundings with pleasant colleagues and interesting equipment. If you think that you might like to do that kind of work some day, here is what you need to do now [in grade school]. Learn to read and write as well as you can. And learn your basic mathematics, arithmetic and especially algebra. Then the doors of opportunity will be open to you.

> Goodbye. Best wishes. Good luck. And take care — of your future.

The Next Step Upward in Higher Education?

You don't really understand something until you can explain it to the man in the street.
PETER DEBYE

A thank you note by a seventh grade teacher regarding a Van Visit, taken with comments regarding participation in Van Visits by two student presenters, suggests what the next step upward in higher education might be.

Wrote the seventh grade teacher (cited previously):

> *"I loved the way you made the kids THINK. No lectures—yea! Your demonstrations were out of sight—all right! If there is one thing my kids love to do it is to <u>think</u>. Thank you for providing them with this marvelous opportunity. <u>Well done</u>!"*

> Two questions encourage kids to think.
> Before execution of a demo, the question:
> *What do you suppose will happen if . . . ?*
> And after execution of a demo without an explanation, the question:
> *"What's going on here?"*

The visit that elicited the seventh grade teacher's endorsement was not made by a Van Program's senior presenters. It was made by two graduate students! They had been with the program for less than a year, at the end of which one of them said:

> **"Running Van Visits was even better than my [PhD] research."**

An undergraduate participant in Van Visits said, similarly, that -

> *"It was the best thing that happened to me at the University this year."*

One wonders:

> *Might higher education aim higher and institutionalize the phenomenon of undergraduate and graduate students becoming proficient with the fundamentals of chemistry — and, also, with speaking effectively in public (deemed by employers of baccalaureate- and PhD-degree chemists to be their chief weakness) — in order to execute safely and to explain correctly and clearly striking demonstration-experiments for younger students, their teachers, and the general public?*

The limiting reagent? Not suitable demonstration-experiments. Not receptive audiences. Not potential student-presenters. Rather — owing to the grant system of support of faculty research and, accordingly, University promotion policies based on faculty success in obtaining research grants with overhead based on published research — the limiting reagent is enthusiastic faculty mentors keen to teach chemistry with their students in the grand inspirational manner from demonstration-experiments.

Personal Note

Henry A. Bent has had the good fortune from the standpoint of teaching chemistry from demonstration-experiments of having had frequent encounters with his audiences' favorite events, the same ones featured in Hollywood action movies: flames and explosions. "Young Henry's" encounters with them have included: lectures in general chemistry by his father, "Big Henry", Henry E. Bent, famous for his demonstration-experiments, particularly his Christmas Lectures on Flames and Explosions; fire-control training in the US Navy during WWII; work on a PhD thesis on the experimental determination of the kinetics and mechanisms of the thermal and explosive decomposition of molten ammonium nitrate; extensive burning of brush in the Northwoods of Minnesota; experimental studies for the Office of Naval Research on the combustion of double-base, nitroglycerin/nitrocellulose propellants for Nike rockets; experimental studies of the thermal decomposition of ditertiary butyl peroxide; forty years of teaching general chemistry from demonstration-experiments, frequently featuring flames and explosions; three years of directing an outreach program based on demonstration-experiments, the most popular of which involved flames and explosions; and for four years execution of Pittsburgh's Faraday Christmas Lectures for science honor students from the tri-state region of western PA, eastern OH, and northern WV, featuring flames and explosions.

Those experiences have convinced him, to paraphrase Faraday, again, that there is not a law under which any part of chemistry is governed nor a phenomenon involved in the harnessing the power of combustion in industry and in our private lives that does not come into play in teaching chemistry from demonstration-experiments featuring Flames and Explosions.

FLAMES AND EXPLOSIONS

Part 2

Henry E. Bent's Last Lecture in Chemistry 1
University of Missouri – Columbia, 1971

Taped by Dr. Bickford. Transcribed by Henry A. Bent

Introduction. "It's a unique day for some of you. I suspect this may be the last chemistry lecture you will hear. It's a unique day for me. It's a last lecture for me in chemistry. So we have a lot in common. I suggest we relax and have a good time. To help you have a good time I have written out your notes for you. That is, in part. If you will pass these back. You may want to take a few notes on some of these pages. They will help you follow the lecture without any need for a lot of writing. Also I want to welcome visitors from chemistry 1 in the other sections, and chemistry 5, and anyone else who happens to be here."

> **H. E. Bent's Lectures** in Chemistry 1 were legendary at the University of Missouri. Graduate students and staff often attended them.

"Today we are going to talk about carbon once more. We've been talking about the methane series, and the fact that those compounds are used as fuels. So then I am going to talk about flames and explosions and the way in which they relate to carbon compounds. I will be doing mostly demonstrations. At the same time you may want to make a few little sketches of the things we will be doing so that you really get the most out of the lecture."

> *Watch, Listen, Write.*

> To obtain additional benefits from the educational experiences that lie latent in demonstration-experiments, follow in the footsteps of Michael Faraday and Dr. Bent.

> *Show. Describe. Explain.*

> Become a member of faculty-mentored student-team motivated to learn chemistry in order to execute safely and to explain correctly striking demonstration-experiments for peers, younger students, and the general public. It's a winner for all lives it touches, especially those of student apprentices. "The best thing that happened to me in school," said one.

Kindling Temperatures. "When we talk about flames, the first thing we have to recognize is that some materials catch fire and burn easily and others have to be heated to a rather high temperature. So I am going to demonstrate that fact with two liquids here that are rather inflammable so that if I should use a match it would not be a very informative experiment because they both catch fire so easily. The general rule is: Never open up a bottle of ether in a laboratory when you have a flame. So that's the first thing we are going to violate here.

"But this is a pretty good-sized room and [based on that observation and my memory of personal experiences] I don't think that it is very dangerous."

Safe Passages through Life = Observation + Knowledge + Memory + Experience + Imagination + Common Sense.

"So I am putting the stopper in promptly and covering what I just poured out into a crystallizing dish with this inverted larger crystallizing dish to diminish ether vapor escaping into the room. This is ordinary ether. This is carbon disulfide. Both are carbon compounds. And now, instead of using a match, which, as I said, wouldn't tell us very much (in as much as the temperature of a match's flame is rather high, perhaps sixteen hundred degrees or so, so that both of these compounds would catch fire readily), I am going to use a cooler ignition source. Perhaps we can turn off the front lights for this experiment. Some of these flames are not very luminous."

> **Alcohol's Low Luminosity Flame.** Friends of the Bents nearly lost a home when their young son tipped over on their back porch an alcohol-burning burner of a chemistry set, righted it, but failed to notice that alcohol was burning, almost invisibly, at first, along the porch wall.

"What I am trying to do here is to heat up a glass rod so that I can have a much lower temperature in order to test the kindling temperature of ether and carbon disulfide. A Pyrex rod at 1600 degrees flows readily as a liquid — in fact, at 400 degrees it begins to get soft, so we know that it is not very hot here in this flame from heating it just this short time."

> **A Glass-Blowing Dean.** Dr. Bent was familiar with the properties of glass, first-hand, as an expert glassblower. In his day researchers in experimental chemistry often constructed much of their own apparatus.
>
> One Christmas he made for his wife from glass tubing an elegantly simple holder for cut flowers, admired by a neighbor who had an eye for objects of art, which she'd acquire on trips to Europe and sell from her home across the street from the Bents in Columbia, Missouri. Dr. Bent obligingly made several blossom holders for his enterprising neighbor, who was soon disappointed, however, that her supplier was too busy as a Graduate Dean and a Professor of Chemistry to meet a large demand for his cut flower holders.

"So, let's try it to see if it is hot enough to ignite the ether or carbon disulfide. And you see that the carbon disulfide ignites readily. The ether does not, sometimes . . . There we are. And here we are with a very low temperature for the glass, so low that I can rub it on my hand without burning it. We say that carbon disulfide has a low kindling temperature. Ether has a higher kindling temperature. Sometimes that is of practical importance."

> **Autoignition Temperatures** are 90°C for carbon disulfide, for ether 160°, for white phosphorus 34°, for gasoline 246-290°, for ethanol 363°, for paper 218-246°, for magnesium 473°, and for hydrogen 536°.
>
> **Living Dangerously?** The cited autoignition temperatures imply that warming in warm water a bottle rocket charged with an oxygen-ethanol vapor mixture would be a safe thing to do, as would warming with a torch to hand-warmth the barrel of a cannon charged with an oxygen-octane mixture, deemed alarming to a group of high school chemistry teachers

and their teachers at a summer institute about chemistry at the University of Wisconsin - Madison.

The most striking and memorable demonstration-experiments are often those that to uninformed eyes, and minds, appear to be dangerous, but that really aren't.

"That's what made them exciting," wrote a middle school student about a program at his school that had featured flames and explosions.

Live dangerously, in view of the uninformed. Lay your life on the line, so far as the untutored can tell. Little ventured by teachers, little gained by students.

A good way to demonstrate confidence in facts and ideas is to do something that would be hazardous to one's health if one's information and reasoning were wrong. Bet your life—or health—that you really do believe that what you are doing and saying is safe. Seek hazardous situations: execution of potentially harmful demonstration-experiments, lecturing without notes, lecturing from students' questions, solving problems at a black or white board without prior practice; in short: *wing it*, in all the ways that you can.

Elevated simultaneously is the quality of education for students and the status of teachers in society. For there's little prestige in doing something that many people believe that they could do equally well.

"At first I was nervous about what you were doing," said a parent at a summer YMCA camp for families regarding an evening of entertainment that featured demonstrations with ethanol, a propane torch, and dry ice. "But then I realized that you seemed to know what you were doing." The program ended with the contents of a 55 gallon G.I. can containing crushed dry ice poured into the base of a camp fire and plastic soft drink bottles charged with crushed dry ice, rowed out into the camp's lake, capped, and tossed over board.

A Simple Hallmark of Expert Teaching exists: How much of an adventure would it be for a non-expert to teach as an expert teacher teaches?

"When I was a student [continues Dr. Bent], there was a professor of English who followed a chemistry class that had ended up one day with some carbon disulfide, thrown down the sink at the end of the lecture bench. When the professor started to lecture he lit a cigarette [this was around 1920] and tossed the match into the sink. Everything that was down there came up in his face and he was aware of the low kindling temperature of carbon disulfide." [Laughter]

Spontaneous Ignition of Yellow Phosphorus. "Here is another substance that has a low kindling temperature: yellow phosphorus It will ignite very readily It is dissolved here in carbon disulfide. So we have two substances that are readily combustible. I will take a little of this solution of phosphorus dissolved in carbon disulfide and dribble it along on this large piece of filter paper. [Brief pause. One infers that Dr. Bent's attention was closely focused for a few moments on handling the yellow-phosphorus-in-carbon-disulfide-solution with *care*.]

THE MERCK INDEX ON YELLOW PHOSPHORUS: Ignites at about 30°C in moist air. *Caution: handle with forceps. Keep under water*. The fumes and the element itself are poisonous. External contact may cause severe burns. Ingestion of even small amounts of yellow phosphorus may produce circulatory collapse, coma, convulsions, and death.

"The carbon disulfide evaporates leaving the phosphorus very finely divided on the filter paper. As you can see, it catches fire spontaneously and comes out as the letter 'P'."

Flame Extinction. "Now we've been hearing more and more today about the wisdom of being able to control our chemical discoveries. So, if we can produce flames, we ought to be able to put them out as well lest they do serious damage. I'm going to use carbon dioxide here as a fire extinguisher. That's rather curious, in a way. We use carbon-containing compounds in combustion. But what better way to put out a fire than a compound of carbon. But after carbon has burned to carbon dioxide, its highest oxide, it can't burn any more. As once said –

'An element's highest oxide can't burn anymore in air than a dead man can die.'

"And so the carbon dioxide we have in this large tank [an aquarium] can be used as a fire extinguisher. Now I'll test to see whether or not the tank is full of carbon dioxide, with this burning splint. You can see that the splint goes out when I plunge it into the tank. So now we'll light the candles on this inclined Plexiglas trough. We could have shown this experiment when we talked about carbon dioxide last week, but it fits in just about as well with flames. And so you can tie it up with either part of our discussion.

> **"Any demo illustrates all of chemistry,"** Professor Lawrence Strong liked to say. "The Tao is hidden in the depths of all things." Every thing is made of atoms. Hence, anything about any thing illustrates something about atoms.

"Now, I dip out with this kitchen pan some carbon dioxide [gentle laughter]. While I'm doing this you are all thinking that the formula of carbon dioxide is CO_2, so that means the molecular weight is 44 — 2 times 16 is 32 and 12 is 44. It's heavier, molecule for molecule, than air.

> **Numbers matter.** 'There is no getting out of it. Through and through the world is infected with quantity. To talk sense is to talk quantities. It's no use saying radium is scarce. How scarce? It's no use saying a nation is large. How large? you may fly to poetry or music, and quantity and number will face you in your rhythms and octaves. Elegant intellects that despise the theory of quantity, are but half developed.' ALFRED NORTH WHITEHEAD
>
> Dalton's Atomic Theory was based on his Law of Multiple *Proportions*. Mendeleev's Periodic Law is based on Atomic *Numbers*. Chemical formulas are relations among *integers*.

"So, I can dip up a dipper here, I hope, of carbon dioxide [chuckling]. Just to keep air currents from blowing it around too much, I'll put a cover on it here and then I can move it over quickly [to our candle trough]. Now we take off our cover and pour carbon dioxide . . . [Laughter. More laughter! Cheers!! Applause!!!]

> **Knowledge for Survival's Sake.** With many audiences it's often easy to get laughter with jokes. Most any joker can do it. And usually it's easy to get cheers and applause with large flames and loud explosions. Almost any person putting on a chemical magic show can do it. But to get all three things — laughter, cheers, applause — at the end of a school

term from a captive audience from merely silent extinction of several candles, without being a comic, or an actor, or a magician, and while not talking about something "relevant", such as "chemistry in the community," "chemistry applied to world needs," or "chemistry and the environment", but, rather, while talking about *pure chemistry* — chemical formulas, molecular weights, and gas densities — illustrates homo *sapiens'* deep-seated desire to know how the world works in order to work with Nature in order to survive in order to contribute to the species' gene pool.

Appeal of Pure and Applied Science for Youngsters. When we began doing demonstration-experiments for school children, we thought that while executing Faraday's experiments with a candle we ought mention uses of carbon black: in car tires, hoses, belts, gaskets, and, valued at hundreds of dollars per pound, in inkjet printers and high performance chromatography columns . . . altogether a multi-billion dollar business. Ho hum. Young people weren't interested. They weren't thinking, yet, about earning a living. What fascinated them was learning that, from the standpoint of combustion, a candle's flame is hollow. "At first I didn't believe a thing you were saying," said a sixth grader. "But if you think about it [the shape of a candle's wick from the standpoint of the Triangle of Fire], it's the truth plain and simple."

The Oxy-Hydrogen Flame. "Now, you've just seen a low temperature flame, with carbon disulfide. Now I want to talk about a high temperature flame. For that purpose I have hydrogen in this tank and oxygen in this tank.

"Hydrogen will burn — let's turn off everything but the backlights — and give a very hot flame. It's a flame that shows a little bit of light because there are little specks of dust — chalk dust and so on from my hands — that get into it. These get hot an give it luminosity. Now, if we introduce oxygen, we get a still hotter flame, because air contains nitrogen, which does not burn. So the nitrogen tends to cool off the flame. But if I use oxygen straight without any nitrogen in it then I don't have that cooling effect due to the nitrogen.

"So, I'm going to turn on the oxygen. Now you see a very hot flame. I can show how hot it is by using it to heat up a bit of copper wire here. The copper heats up to something like a thousand degrees, melts, and drips off the end of the copper wire [into a beaker of water?].

> **Temperature-Limiting Thermal Decomposition of Products of Combustion.** The oxy-hydrogen flame is famous for melting platinum (mp 1772°C). It is not nearly as hot, however, as it would be if all of the heat of the exothermic reaction $H_2 + 1/2\ O_2 = H_2O$, *going to completion*, heated up the molecules of water formed. That would yield a flame temperature above 5000°C. In fact, the maximum temperature of an oxy-hydrogen flame is about 2600°C, because the hydrogen-oxygen reaction does not go to completion at high temperatures owing, at high temperatures, to decomposition of H_2O.
>
> **Nature's Hottest Flame** is produced by combustion in oxygen of cyanogen, NCCN, yielding Nature's strongest bonds: the triple bonds of NN and CO.
>
> $$NCCN + OO = NN + CO$$
>
> Cyanogen's combustion is not as exothermic as hydrogen's combustion, but its flame temperature is about 4500°C.

Luminosity. "Well, so much for the variation of flame temperatures. Now lets turn to the matter of luminosity.

Lime Light. "The same torch will give what I want here: a nonluminous but very hot flame only luminous when there is a solid object in it, like chalk dust, which can get very hot [without vaporizing] and then the chalk dust gives off light. This was the first very bright light, created for theatrical purposes, only instead of using chalk dust they used a little piece of quicklime. Now quicklime is calcium oxide and, again, calcium oxide can't burn anymore because its calcium has already burned. It has all the oxygen that it can combine with.

> **Quicklime from Chalk.** Each of the thousands points of light when chalk dust (finely divided calcium carbonate) gets into an oxy-hydrogen flame (where it decomposes to lime and carbon dioxide) is a tiny source of limelight.
>
> Calcium carbonate ($CaCO_3$, aka limestone) + heat = Calcium oxide (CaO, aka lime) + CO_2

"And so I direct this very hot flame toward the quicklime . . . Let's turn down the lights. Don't look directly at this because it's pretty bright. But if you look at the room you can get some idea of how much light is given off . . . All right, can we have the lights?

"This light that you just saw can be focused with a lens down onto the platform of a theatre. It's called "limelight". So, for once, you've been in the limelight, if you've never been in it before.

> **Hot-Solid-Body Light.** Limelight is an instance of hot-solid-body light. Other instances are magnesium flares, candles, and incandescent lights.
>
> | Type of Light | Hot Solid | Enabling Chemical Reaction |
> | --- | --- | --- |
> | Limelight | Calcium Oxide | Combustion of Hydrogen with Oxygen |
> | Candlelight | Soot | Combustion of Candle Wax with air |
> | Magnesium Flare | Magnesium Oxide | Combustion of Magnesium with air |
> | Incandescent Light | Tungsten Filament | Combustion of Fossil Fuel at a Power Plant |
>
> Hot-solid-body light is called in physics "black body radiation". Black bodies absorb, and emit, light of all frequencies. To describe the dependence of the intensity of the radiation on its frequency and on the temperature of the black body, Max Planck was forced to suppose, for the first time in the history of human thought, that energy is quantized.
>
> Planck was not immediately in the limelight. Few physicists knew much about black body radiation. Then, a dozen or so years later, Einstein used Planck's quantum hypothesis to account for diamond's anomalous specific heat; and every physicist knew what specific heat is. Soon they were calling the leading physical constant of quantum physics "Planck's Constant".

"Well, so much for flames as far as luminosity is concerned . . . except we might want to check this a little bit. [Here Dr. Bent recovers smoothly from near omission of an experiment he'd planned to do.]

"If what we said is correct, then I ought to be able to destroy the luminosity of a flame by cooling it down, shouldn't I? So let's try that here with an experiment that is not very dramatic, but it checks our theory, perhaps, if it works. Here we have methane burning with not enough air to burn up all its carbon and hydrogen. So here the solid particles that give off light are hot carbon particles. If they are not hot enough, of course, they will not give off light.

"So, let's turn off the front lights again. And I am going to try and hold this copper sheet in such a way as to cool down the flame, for copper is a very good conductor of heat. And you can see what it does to the luminosity. I won't hold it in the flame very long because, of course, if the copper gets hot, and I can feel that it is, it doesn't do it job so well, and, further, becomes too hot to hold. So, I will hold it here for just a second or so and you can see that most of the luminosity has disappeared.

> **A Verbal Tick of Dr. Bent's Commentaries.** Unlike sentences in chemical magic shows, sentences in commentaries on demonstration-experiments that *tell a story* in which each experiment follows logically from the previous experiment and leads logically to the next experiment frequently begin with such words as "So," "Now", "If," "Then;" and "Well".

A Flame and a Flask in Free and Rapidly Arrested Fall. "Now I want to do an experiment which gives us a better idea of the way in which combustion takes place. I need a little help with this. I have a volunteer here."

Use of Student Volunteers –

- Demonstrates that Nature is lawful. She always does here thing. There is no sleight-of-hand in demonstration-experiments. Almost any interested person can be a scientist.

- Increases audience interest in outcomes of an experiment — which, were Nature not lawful, might not "work" (as expected).

- Sends the message that participation in science is socially acceptable.

- Increases participants' self-esteem, by helping to execute something significant in science before an audience of appreciative peers and adults.

"I am going to light these two candles in these two flasks. The victim will sit down here in front of us. [Laughter] I am keeping one of these candles simply for control, so that you can see that there is sufficient air in one of these stoppered flasks to support combustion for quite a while. The other one we will play around with here. I am going to ask our victim to catch it as I am going to drop it. And if he misses it you will know what that means for his final grade. [Laughter]

"So, I will light these two candles."

> **One Way to Ignite a Candle in a Flask** is to weld the candle, held vertical mechanically, to the flask, with candle wax, by warming, momentarily, the bottom of the flask. Then rotate the flask until the candle is horizontal. And, finally, ignite the candle with a burning splint taped to a second splint.

"Now, with the candle down inside the flask it is protected from air currents. I can swing it around you see and toss it up and down with no effect on the flame because air currents can't get to it. I'm going to ask you to guess if you can what's going to happen if I drop it. Of course, it might break. But we'll assume that it won't. So . . . Hold your hands pretty low. I'm going to drop it from up here and you see what happens when he catches it. [Laughter] Ready? . . . *The flame went out before the flask reached his hand* [emphasis added]. Thank you very much. We'll raise your grade one letter." [Laughter]

> **Audience Punctuations of Lectures.** Laughter — to paraphrase Oscar Wilde — is not a bad way to begin a demo, and it is far the best way to end one. "They love him," said a friend as he and a visitor passed a lecture hall at Columbia University in which one of Dr. Bent's grandsons, Brian E. Bent, a demo-doer, was lecturing to a class of general chemistry students who were laughing. By-products of interesting demos are smiles, clapping, and cheers; and, of apt remarks, laughter.

"Now, the interesting question: Why did the flame go out."

Reasons that Have Been Offered for Extinction of a Flame in a Flask that Has Been Dropped and Caught

- Air is sucked out of the flask (if it's not stoppered).
- The flame falls through a layer of carbon dioxide.
- Free fall produces a shock wave that extinguishes the flame (suggested by a physical chemist)

"It certainly was not a breeze, was it? Because the cool air outside the flask can't get close to the wick."

> **Beware of "Certainly"** — and "clearly"; and such phrases as "of course" and "it's obvious that . . ." Sometimes it's not.

"Well, if you stop to think, a candle burning is really a more complex phenomenon — it's still burning in this other flask — than one might think at first glance. What's happening is that the products of combustion are *hot*. By the gas laws, that means that they expand [at constant pressure]. The density is less, and fresh air comes in. How is that different when we drop a candle? We're getting the same products. They're still hot. But now there's no effect due to gravity. Because a freely falling body acts as if there were no gravity at all. That is what happens in space ships, you know, when passengers float around in space."

> **As Einstein liked to point out:** You can't "drop" anything in a freely falling elevator. It's as if gravity were turned off. Everything (Galileo discovered) falls (in a vacuum) at the same rate.

"So, as a result, it doesn't make any difference whether the gas around the candle is light or heavy. There's no way for it to get away. There's no buoyant effect which causes the hot combustion products to rise and bring in fresh air. So this candle smothers simple because there was no force of gravity to make the lighter, hot gases rise.

"You might be amused that when we first talked about trying this experiment we had the idea that we might have to go to the local TV station and drop it from the top of its tower. That was ambitious, of course, and my colleague Dr. Thomas said, "Why don't you just drop it 30 feet down an empty elevator shaft in the old chemistry building?" Well, we did that and then we said maybe we don't have to drop it that far. So we ended up dropping it three feet here."

Unexpected Sequels to the Candle-in-Free-Fall Experiment

Scientific Theories Live Dangerously. They can be disproved, by experiments. It's their distinctive feature. Undisprovable theories — God Exists, e.g. — are not scientific theories.

One Experiment Too Many for the Smothering Theory of Flame Extinction in Free Fall. If the Smothering Theory is correct, a toss *upward* of three feet or so of the candle and flask, followed by further gravity-free motion downward, should extinguish the flame. It doesn't!

Additional Tests of the Flame-Smothering Theory. In the 1960's, NASA, responding to criticisms regarding a paucity of scientific experiments in its expensive space program, solicited suggests for such experiments.

> Take a candle into space, suggested your author.

> *No thanks!* Not after the fatal fire in an oxygen-pressurized capsule awaiting launch at Cape Canaveral.

On second thought, though: perhaps it would be wise to know how flames behave in space. So NASA built a "microgravity" facility, described below in its own words.

"The NASA Glen 2.2-Second [evacuated] Drop Tower is one of two drop towers located at the NASA Site in Brookpark, Ohio. The tower, which began life as a 100-foot high fuel distillation tower, dangles over a bluff at the Glenn Research Center. The tower has been used for nearly 50 years by researchers from around the world to study the effects of microgravity on physical phenomena such as combustion and fluid dynamics, and to develop new technology for space missions.

" Microgravity, which is a condition of (near) weightlessness, can only be achieved on or near Earth by putting an object in a state of free fall. In this way, NASA conducts microgravity experiments on Earth using drop towers and aircraft flying parabolic maneuvers, and in space using unmanned rockets, the Space Shuttle, and the International Space Station.

"The 2.2-Second Drop Tower is 'a gateway to space' for many of the microgravity experiments conducted on the Space Shuttle and the International Space Station because these experiments often begin on Earth with exploratory testing in the drop tower. This may be followed by further drop testing to verify or optimize the design of the space hardware and to identify the best test conditions for the space experiment. As such the drop tower is used to maximize the scientific return from experiments conducted in space. This is an important role, given the significant investment required to conduct space experiments in both time and money.

"The drop tower's 2.2 second test time is created by allowing the experiment package to free fall a distance of 79 feet (24 m). $[(1/2)gt^2 = (1/2)(32 \text{ ft/sec}^2)(2.2 \text{ sec})^2 = 77 \text{ ft.}]$ The Drop Tower uses a drag shield system to minimize the aerodynamic drag on the free falling experiment. Experiments are assembled in a rectangular aluminum frame which is enclosed in aerodynamically designed drag shield (which weighs 725 pounds). This package is hoisted to the top of the tower (the eighth floor), where it is connected to monitoring equipment (e,g,, high speed video cameras and on board computers) before being dropped. A low gravity environment is created as the package free falls from the eighth floor to the first floor, a distance of 79 feet 1 inch. The experiment is isolated from aerodynamic drag because it is not attached to the drag shield. The experiment itself falls seven and one half inches within the drag shield while the entire package is falling. The drop ends when the drag shield and experiment are stopped by an air bag at the bottom of the tower."

The Results, with Candle Flames? They become smaller during free fall. And nearly spherical. *But they don't out!*

Conclusion. Extinction of a candle's flame occurs after free fall that is followed *immediately* by its *sudden arrestment.*

Revised Flame Extinction Theory. What happens the moment the candle-containing flask is caught is that, in the candle's frame of reference, gravity is suddenly turned back on. Suddenly buoyancy comes into play. Suddenly hot combustion products are displaced upward by inrushing, denser, colder air, from all directions, cooling the wick. Suddenly vaporization of fuel ceases. Suddenly the flame goes out, blown out, so to speak, without a flicker, by an unusual "breeze".

A Test of the Revised Flame Extinction Theory: Arrest a falling candle and flask *slowly*, by attaching the flask to, e.g., a slinky, and dropping it from a height such that it comes to rest before it hits a floor.

Done, in a pubic lecture at Purdue University in a large auditorium that has a balcony. The result? *The flame didn't go out.*

Moral, regarding H. E. Bent's flame-extinction theory (held, also, initially, by his son, H. A. Bent): One tends to see what one expects to see.

Given freedom to experiment, however, science tends to be self-correcting.

An Inverted Flame. "Well, the next thing we want to do is to inquire a little bit more about the nature of combustion. Here's an apparatus I should probably draw, although it is extremely simple. In fact, you can do it: a tube with a short side tube and smaller diameter ones entering and exiting the larger tube through one-hole stoppers.

"This gives me the opportunity to run natural gas, methane, in the side and have it rise out the top because methane is less dense than air. [Slight pause while the side tube is connected to a gas jet.] Well, I turn on the gas and as you expect it rises and I can ignite it at the top of the apparatus. If I have enough gas pressure, it can't all exit at the top and some will emerge from the bottom, where it can be lit, also. So now I have methane flowing out and burning at both ends of the tube. Now, let's turn off the lighs. I turn off the gas. And now you can see a little flame inside, as air enters at the bottom and burns in an atmosphere of methane.

"Here, at the top, we have methane burning in air and here inside we have air burning in methane. The same chemical reaction is occurring at both locations. Inside, what we call the 'atmosphere' is methane, outside it's air.

"So this gives us a little more of an idea of what we mean by combustion. It might seem like a cheap way of getting energy, just burn air. But, of couse, you have to keep supplying gas to keep the air burning. Lights please.

A Bunsen Burner's Flame. "Now we want to turn to our most common flame in the laboratory: the Bunsen burner's flame. In a Bunsen burner we have a tube with holes at the bottom so that air can enter and mix with fuel entering through a small opening at the bottom. And then we have a cone and a seond cone above it."

Connical Flame Fronts arise from a mechanical phenomenon: viscous drag. Gas flow is zero in a boundary layer and increaes toward the middle of the tube.

"You've all played with Bunsen burners and are familiar with this structure. Now what we want to find out is what happens in different parts of the flame."

Truth-Seeking. "We come here to be philosophers," Faraday liked to say of his lectures for juvenal audienes at England's Royal Institution. Dr. Bent was of the same mind-set with regard to his student audiences at the University of Missouri. High expectations engender responsible behavior.

One morning in an all-day visit to a middle school, the author encountered an audience of giddy boys and girls. "O.K.," he said, going to Plan B. "That's it for this morning. Perhaps we can execute our most striking flames and explosions on another occasion, when you are prepared to pay attention." During the subsequent break in presentations, teachers let their visitor know that they felt that he was being unduely harsh. Well, whatever. Thereafter, the school's audiences were as quiet as church mice.

"Kids are like puppies." Dr. Bent's second son used to say. "They'll take all the leash you give them." They may be just as happy, however, on a short leash as on a long leash — indeed, perhaps even happier, as it's a constant reminder of a loving link with the leash-holder.

"Why [now] is the inner cone blue and the outer one more diffuse and a slightly different color?

As we'll see, the fuel in the inner and outer cones isn't the same.

"Well, an interesting way of exploring the Bunsen burner's flame is to take a piece of asbestos paper. Asbestos paper doesn't burn. And so If I put this flame at a angle and hold the asbestos paper in it for a few moments you see what happens. I get a charring around here and in the center of the eliptical charred region, where I'm touching it, it's perfectly cold. Around the outside, however, I'm not going to touch it because that is charred and quite hot. The charring shows what is happening in the flame.

"It's cold here in the center but its hotter around the outside. So that means there is no reaction taking place inside the inner cone. It's cold, What happens is that gas already mixed with air burns in part [the mixture Is fuel rich] over the surface of the inner cone and then the rest goes up higher, where it mixes eventually, with air, and burns over the surface of the upper cone, as a diffusion flame."

Strike back? The flame of the gas mixture does not strike back to the base of the burner, where the air and gas inlets are, so long as the gas flow-rate upward is greater than the flame's burning velocity downward.

"If what I have said is true, I should be able to take a match here and put it inside the inner cone and not have it ignite. So I'll try this. I've put a little pin throug the match stick. And sure enough, the match stick does not ignite even though it is inside the flame. So, of course, whenever you are using a Bunsen burner to heat an object, you keep it above the inner cone. Of course, you may think this is a dummy match and won't burn. So I'll more it over to the side. And you see it catches fire."

Wordsmiths. Apt descriptions and explanations of experiments have a poetic quality. When asked why he attended Sir Humphrey Davy's lectures at the Royal Institution, Coleridge said: "to renew my stock of metaphors."

Smithells Description of a Bunsen Burner's Flame. "One way to form a flame is to allow the whole of one gas, mixed with a less quantity of a second gas than is sufficient for complete combustion, to issue into the second. This is the case with what are generally known as atmospheric burners, of which the Bunsen burner is the prototype. The development of a flame of this type can be well studied in the case of carbon monoxide and air. The carbon monoxide is fed into a Bunsen burner with closed air valves. The flame consists of a single conical blue sheet. If now the air valves be opened slightly, an internal cone of the same color makes its appearance. The air which has entered through the air valves ('primary air') has mixed with the carbon monoxide and so oxidizes its quota in an internal cone. The rest of the carbon monoxide (diluted now, of course, with carbon dioxide and nitrogen) wanders into the external air to burn (with 'secondary air') in a second cone" [in which, again, the fuel, as mentioned, is carbon monoxide].

Smithells' Separator. "Well, a man named Smithells a good many years ago developed this apparatus for studying these cones and that's the next thing I want to play with."

> **Laughter Errupted** in a middle school science class, unexpectedly, for a visiting scientist, following his remark that "we will now play around with [something or other]". Evidently the students did not expect to hear in a science class the word "play".

"I have here a little pilot light so that I don't have to keep lighting a match or something every time my flame goes out. Oops. I just did what I guess every beginning instructor does. I connected the tube to the burner to the air jet. [Laughter] That's not as bad as connecting it to the water jet. [Loud laughter]

> **Fieser's Lecture on Lab Safety.** One of Dr. Bent's young colleagues at Harvard University, with whom he used to play squash, the later famous organic chemist Louie Fieser, used to give a popular lecture in the grand inspirational manner in which he demonstrated for his students nearly every mistake he'd ever seen made in a student organic lab. Included were charcoal spills, ether fires, and the hooking up of a Bunsen burner to a cold water faucet. It was Fieser's distinctive teaching style, for promoting lab safety.
>
> **Style,** says Alfred North Whitehead, is, in its finest sense, "the last acquirement of the educated mind . . . [It] is always the exclusive privilege of the expert. Who ever heard of the style of an amateur painter, or the style of an amateur poet. Style is always the product of specialist study, the peculiar contribution of specialism to culture."

"Now, I have a big Bunsen burner down at the bottom of this big glass tube here. And I'll turn it on. The glass tube simply conveys the gas up to its top end, where I can ignite it, and you can see the flame readily. Now, can I have all the lights off. Here's our Bunsen flame with the inner cone not very visible. I'll let in a little more air. There, we have a nice blue cone. Now, what's happening here is that the gas and air are burning, but they are burning so slowly that the flame does not travel down the tube.

"If I slow down the speed with which the gases are going up the large glass tube above the large Bunsen burner, then it's possible for the flame to travel down. You see there is a competition here between how fast the gas is flowing up and how fast the flame burns downward. So I'll cut down on the gas a bit and see if I can get the inner cone to come down. . . Now I've got a smaller tube in the middle here, which has the effect of speeding the gas flow. Now I'm slowing it down some more. . . There we are!

"Now we have the two cones separated. You can't see the upper one very well because its pretty cool. And now if we want we can take gas out of the intermediate gas space and see what's happened. What's the product of combustion in this lower cone, which I like to call the explosion zone, although it doesn't make any noise. No bang. But it's a mixture of gases that is capable of exploding under the right conditions.

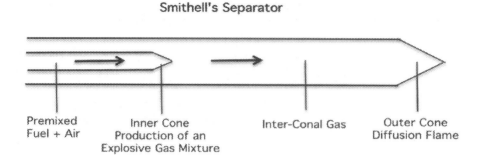

Smithell's Separator

Premixed
Fuel + Air

Inner Cone
Production of an
Explosive Gas Mixture

Inter-Conal Gas

Outer Cone
Diffusion Flame

"Let's turn up the speed a little bit and chase the inner cone back up, just so you can see that we can move it either way. Right now we've got an unstable condition, where it oscillates. It's a temptation to do this for a long time, but we'll stop soon [chuckles].

"Now I've got it going pretty fast, so that the inner cone cannot travel down. The shape of the inner cone is, of course, a result of the fact that the gas at the center of the tube is going faster than the gas at the edges. We'd have a perfectly horizontal flame front were it not for that difference in speeds. But in the center of the flame the higher gas speed "pushes up" the flame, so to speak, and makes the flame front pointed. Well, let's turn on the lights.

"An equation for what is happening starts with methane and oxygen and should show, according to Smithell's data, formation of carbon monoxide and hydrogen.

$$CH_4 + O_2 = CO + H_2$$

"I don't need to balance the equation for an experienced group like this. And, anyway, it's only an approximate sketch of what happens."

> **Smithell's Data** for the inter-conal gas of methane burning in air, in percentages by volume, which, by Avogadro's Law, are also molecular percentages, are:
>
> CO 4.5 CO_2 6.8 H_2 3.2 H_2O 17.6 N_2 67.2
>
> Checks: (1) Since the only source of H and C atoms is CH_4, the ratio of H to C atoms should be 4. And -
>
> (2) Since the only source of N and O atoms is air, the ratio N to O atoms should be 78/21 = 3.71.
>
> Calc'd: (1) H/C: (2x3.2 + 2x17.6)/(4.5 + 6.8) = 41.6/11.3 = 3.68 (theory: 4.0)
>
> (2) N/O: (2x67.2)/(4.5 + 2x6.8 + 27.6) = 134.4/41.2 = 3.62 (theory: 3.71)

"With an insufficient amount of oxygen, we get two gases that are combustible: carbon monoxide and dihydrogen. So, that means that after those gases go up to the top and get more oxygen from the surrounding air, then you get from the carbon monoxide carbon dioxide and from the hydrogen water.

"Now, a very practical application of all of this.

Davy's Safety Lamp. "We saw that the gas flame could not travel down if the speed of the gas going up was faster than the speed of the flame. This gave rise to a very important invention in England over a century ago, the so called Davy Safety Lamp. This is a lamp taken down into coal mines to protect miners from explosions [of air containing methane, a.k.a. "firedamp"]. There had been many mine explosions and horendous losses of life because of an inability to detect gases that are explosive.

"Here is the Davy Safety Lamp. What is it? Well, it's a little kerosine lamp with a wire gauze. I can illustrate its behavior with a Bunsen burner, if we turn off the lights once more. I take this wire gauze [about 4"x4"] and put it over the flame."

> **A Candle's Flame** serves equally well.

"Of course, through the holes in the wire gauze the gas is going faster."

> Dr. Bent does not explain why that is so. His phrase "of course" is often, in a logical discussion, a red flag, signalling an unsupported assumption.

"So, I can slide this wire gauze over here and pick the flame right off the burner; then put it back down again. Or I can pick it up and throw it away, *because the flame can not pass through the wire gauze, into combustible gas*" [emphasis added].

> **Playing Around with Wire Gauze and a Candle's Flame.**
>
> - With gauze (or a wire screen) placed, horizontal, immediately above a candle's wick, one sees that a candle's diffusion flame is, with respect to combustion, *hollow.*
>
> - With the gauze across the tip of a candle's flame, black, unburnt smoke (soot) rises, owing to a quenching, by cooling, of flame reactions by the metallic, heat-removing wire gauze.
>
> - With the gauze across the flame immediately above the wick (again), rising smoke is white, from condensation of *wax vapor.*
>
> In all instances, it seems that a flame's hot gases do not emerge from passage through a heat-conducting metal gauze with the gases sufficiently hot to initiate combustion. Placed in a flame, a metal gauze quenches whatever high-temperature chemical or physical processes may be occurring at its location.

"Well, that is the principle, then, of the Davy Safety Lamp. It has a wire gauze around the flame so that if you take it into a mine the lamp's hot combustion products will not ignite combustible (or explosive) mine gas.

"I will ignite first this little kerosine lamp and then put the wire gauze around it. And then if you will join me into a trip into a coal mine . . . I wasn't exactly born in a coal mine, but I spent many of my early years in one . . . now we will imagine we're down in a coal mine and here [from this tank of methane] is some gas that has come out of the coal. Watch the flame and see what happens as I squirt methane at it: a little pop shows that you are in some danger, that there is some methane in the mine air. But the methane-containing air did not ignite, except inside the lamp.

"So, if I just squirt [again] a little methane at the lamp, you can tell from the way the flame behavies whether or not it is a dangerous situation and one should get out of the mine before any damage has been done. Of course, it I have a lot of methane, it may burn so effectively, inside the lamp, that it may put the kerosine's flame out. So there would be a case where I'd be using methane as a fire extinguisher, by putting out a flame with it."

An Acetylene Torch in Bad Air. During the Second World War, the author's father-in-law (later), Edwin (Mac) McKnight, a geologist with the U.S. Geological Survey, examined abandoned lead-zinc mines in the Ozarks of Missouri and Arkansas to determine whether or not the mines might be reopened in the war effort. It was dangerous work, owing, in part, to carbon dioxide, from decaying support-timbers, pooling in low areas.

For illumination Mac's young colleagues used electric torches. Mac used an old-fashioned acetylene torch. It produces illumination through formation of a highly sooty flame, from combustion of acetylene (C_2H_2), produced by dropping water onto calcum carbide (CaC_2).

$$CaC_2(s) + 2 H_2O(l) = Ca(OH)_2(s) + C_2H_2(g)$$

One time Mac saved his own life and that of a young colleague who, crawling ahead of Mac in a passageway only a few feet high, had passed out owing to a high concentration of carbon dioxide, signaled to Mac by the behavior of his torch's diffusion flame, as it became longer and longer in search of oxygen in the carbonated air. The phenomenon can be illustrated by playing around with a candle and a drinking glass.

A Candle's Flame in Bad Air. A drinking glass inverted over a candle's flame illustrates the flame-elongating effect of bad air on a diffusion flame. Hold the rim of the drinking glass at about the midpoint of the flame. Check, afterwards, the flammability of the glass's contents with a burning match.

Explosions. I. Aluminum Powder Mixed with Oxygen. "Now, to show you another aspect of flames, I'm going to mix aluminum powder here with oxygen. And I guess that you all know that aluminum doesn't burn very readily. In fact, in air you don't have to worry about it at all. But with aluminum finely divided with a lot of surface sometimes we're able to get it to ignite in oxygen, even though each small particle has a tightly-adhering, protective coat of aluminum oxide. So, I'll mix thoroughly and see what happens. But before I start this I want to test to see if I've expelled all the air in this sturdy metal pipe. I can do that with a glowing splint. If this pipe contains pure oxygen, the glowing splint will be ignited. There. That looks pretty good, doesn't it?"

The Glowing Splint Test for Oxygen. Berzelius, one of the founding fathers of modern chemistry, wrote, on first collecting oxygen: *"I have seldom experienced such a moment of such pure and deep happiness as when the glowing stick which was thrust into the oxygen lighted up and illuminated with unaccustomed brilliancy my windowless laboratory."*

The glowing splint test for oxygen illustrates beautifully the effect of reagent concentration on speeds of chemical transformations. With an ever-present possibility of forest fires started by lightening, mankind — and old-growth forests — are fortunate that the planet's amosphere is merely 21 percent oxygen.

Determination of the dependence of rates of chemical reactions on reagents' concentrations yields information regarding mechanisms of chemical reactions.

Back now to Dr. Bent.

"I'll add just a little bit more oxygen for good measure. Let's turn off all but the back lights. Now I'll shake this up to get a good mixture. Pooop! {Audience Chatter} Ha Ha."

Enjoyment Principle. Enjoyment is contagious. With his "Ha Ha" Dr. Bent was like the four musicians of the St. Lawrence Quartet: "remarkable not merely for the quality of their music-making, exalted as it is, but for the joy they take in the act of connection [with an audience], *The New Yorker*, May 21, 2001, p106.

Explosions. II. Lycopodium Powder with Oxygen. "Now, you know that sometimes experiments don't work [as expected]. So I always have this next experiment as a standby. This is lycopodium powder, from a plant, very finely divided. And although my aluminum frequently does not ignite, I've never had this one fail [to perform as expected]. The lycopodium powder is a little finer than the aluminum powder. And being finer, it burns faster. And in burning faster, you know what . . . So, I'll give this [our combustion chamber] a chance to fill up with oxygen, and while it's doing that, I'll talk about my last experiment."

Trying to fill a container rapidly with gas at high pressure in a tank with a blast of the gas from the tank creates turbulance that sweeps in air, hence the need, if one wishes to avoid that phenomenon, of bleeding the gas into one's container *slowly*. Once the author failed to do so, with oxygen and a beaker, in a public lecture at Purdue University. Fortunately the splint test was applied, before attempting to proceed. Afterwards several people said — as has happened not infrequently on such occasions — that that was the best part of the program: finding out about the oxygen in the beaker.

"The finer the particles the more rapid the reaction. For obviously the reaction takes place on the surface. And so the more surface area there is the quicker the reaction can take place."

It's why we have jaws and teeth, to hasten digestion of solid food.

"What's the finest we can get? Well, we can keep grinding what we're grinding finer and finer. But the finest we can get is to get down to molecules, isn't it? So if I mix molecules as I will here in this bell jar, then we can expect the most rapid reaction we can get.

"So let's test again to see if we have oxygen in our pipe, with lycopodium powder. That looks pretty good. Let's turn out the lights. Those in the front row have a special advantage in these experiments. Are you ready? [Flash of light! Boom! Audience chatter.]

Federal Regulations Regarding Dust. Disasterous dust explosions in mills throughout the United States have led to strict federal regulations enforced by federal inspectors regarding permissable amounts of dust acccumulation on flat surfaces in manufacturing facilities. Issues of life-and-death are often regulated by the federal government.

The Lycopodium-Oxygen Bottle Rocket. In a dust explosion in a pipe, the pipe-holder may notice, in addition to an audience's reaction, the pipe's reaction to the rapid exit from the pipe of hot combustion products. Momentum is conserved. To demonstrate the principle for an audience, decrease the mass of the reaction vessel and the restraining forces acting on it.

Replace, for instance, the pipe by a light, plastic, pop bottle. The demo is best executed outside or in auditoriums or gymnasiums with high ceilings. It works best with two persons: one to shake vigorously a pop bottle charged with oxygen and lycopodium power before placing it immediately on a launching rod; the other to bring the flame of a propane torch taped to a pole quickly to the mouth of the bottle. BOOM! goes the dust explosion. VROOM! goes the bottle.

Harnesed by our engine — the bottle (which usually escapes largely unscathed) — is the power of a spontaneous event: combustion of lycopodium powder. Produced is a "useful effect": visible motion of a ponderable body (the bottle); and, also, excitement and enlightenment in audiences, of all ages. "Do it again!" they say. With more finely divided fuels? Say hydrogen gas; and vapors of rubbing alcohol, diethyl ether, and acetone (the explosion may shatter the rocket); and those fuel/oxygen mixtures at different temperatures?

The chemical bottle rocket can illustrate many things. It's good preparation for discussions of various aspects of organic and physical chemistry, rocket science, and safety. How efficient, for instance, is the rocket engine in converting chemical energy into mechanical energy? (Not very. Haste makes waste, entropy, and thermal pollution.)

"One reason for doing these experiments [continues Dr. Bent] is to get ready for this one." [Audience Chatter]

Explosions. III. Hydrogen in a Bell Jar. "Here is a bell jar that, like a bell, has a large open end, as you can see. At the opposite end is a small opening with a one-hole rubber stopper in it through which runs a small hollow glass tube. Now I will fill it with hydrogen, from a tank, through this rubber tube that I'll run to the top of the bell jar. The important thing at this stage of the experiment is to be sure that all of the air is out of the bell jar.

"I can tell pretty well when the air is all out by the feeling of it. Because hydrogen molecules, being very light and, therefore, moving about relatively rapidly, diffuse relatively quickly, which means that it feels cold to me if I put my hand up into the bell jar, even though the hydrogen, like the air in the room, is at room temperature, since it carries heat away from my warmer hand faster than air does. Now, I am going to play safe and keep running the hydrogen in a bit longer, so that I'm sure I've gotten rid of the air. If any of you in the front row want to move, it's all right as far as I'm concerned. [Delayed laughter]. I see some of you trust me."

> **A Classic Test for the Absence of Air in Hydrogen** consists in running a sample of the gas into a small inverted test tube and exposing its open end to a flame. A slight pop indicates an absence of an explosive mixture.

"I'm going to turn off the hydrogen now and ignite the hydogen exiting through the small glass tube at the top. You can't see anything — or very little — because hydrogen, not containing any carbon, burns with a nearly nonluminous flame. The only product of its combustion is water, which exists in the flame as colorless water vapor.

There's a complete absence in the flame of solid particles, except for a small amount of dust.

"Well, but what we're seeing contradicts what I've just said, because you can see the flame at the end of the *glass* tube, which is getting hot. At first it was cold. But now the glass tubing is hot. There's sodium in it, which, when hot, radiates visible light in the yellow region of the electromagnetic spectrum, giving luminosity to the flame."

Flame Spectrocospy. The ancients knew that sea salt imparts a yellow color to flames. To study flames' colors, Bunsen developed a burner, the Bunsen burner, that produces a nearly colorless flame. With it Bunsen and Kirkhoff discovered in 1860 and 1861 two new elements, named for the colors they impart to flames: cesium "because of its beautiful blue spectral line;" and rubidium because of the "magnificent dark red color of rays" from flames containing its salts (usually relatively volatile chlorides).

Soon thereafter the new method of "atomic spectroscopy" led to the discovery by other investigators of two additional elements: thallium, named for its green spectral line; and indigo, named for its brilliant indigo spectral line. David Alter, of Freeport, Pennsylvania, had shown earlier, in 1854, that each element has its own flame spectrum. He fashioned the light-dispersing glass prism for his spectroscope from a mass of brilliantly clear glass found in a pot of a glass factory destroyed in the great Pittsburgh fire of 1845.

Today the world's leading scientific convention for the introduction of new spectroscopic and other analytical instrumentation is run by SSP, the Spectroscopy Society of Pittsburgh, and SACP, the Society of Analytical Chemists of Pittsburgy, sponsors of Pittsburgy's Faraday Christmas Lectures, offered four times by Dr. Bent's son, Henry A. Bent.

Robert Bunsen. In the 1920s, Dr. Bent studied for his PhD thesis, at the University of California – Berkeley, the thermodynamic properties of Bunsen's cesium. His research advisor was legendary Joel Hildebrand, a founding member of the Sierra Club, coach of an Olymbic ski team, and famous among students at Berkeley for teaching general chemistry in the "grand inspirational manner", from demonstration-experiments. His advice to Dick Powell, HAB's PhD advisor at Berkeley, who, on one occasion, was substituting for Hildebrand in general chemistry, was for him to say, when introducing a demo, not "Now I will show you [such and such]" but, rather, "Let's see what happens when . . ."

When Dr. Bent left Berkeley for his first position in academia, at Harvard University, Hildebrand gave him permission to copy down directions for his lecture demonstrations. Some of them may be in this book. And Hildebrand was not the first person to use them. As a young man he had studied under famous chemists and chemical educators in Europe, some of whom taught chemistry in the "grand inspirational manner", from demonstration-experiments.

Like Dr. Bent, Bunsen's favorite recreation after long days in the laboratory was walking. At age 79 Dr. Bent completed a 50 mile walk one day in under 12 hours. During intermission at a concert that evening, a friend asked him how the walk had gone. "I completed it in 11 hours, 59 minutes, and 45 seconds," said Dr. Bent. "Oh, that's too bad," said his friend's wife, "I would have thought you could have walked another 15 seconds."

Like Dr. Bent, Bunsen was exceedingly modest. Bunsen won many honors and medals. "Such things were of value to me," he once said sadly, "only because they pleased my mother; she is now dead." Bunsen's students were proud of his achievements. When he found it necessary to mention his own discoveries in his lectures, he'd say, not "I have discovered," but, rather, "Man hat gefunden." And his students would respond with prolongued applause.

Bunsen never married. When asked why, he'd say, "I never could find time." Perhaps for that reason his students were especially dear to him, for it's said that he used to work all day in the laboratory patiently showing them the fine details of chemical manipulations.

Bunsen had a vivid imagination. "Every phenomenon embraced for him an endless diversity of factors," it's been said, "and in the yellow flame of an ordinary alcohol lamp whose wick was sprinkled with salt, he saw the possibiity [since realized] of accomplishing the chemical analysis of the most distant stars."

"Now, as this experiment proceeds [continues Dr.Bent] I hope you'll use your imagination and think of what is happening in the bell jar."

Imagination in Art and Science. "I don't render the visible," said Paul Klee, "I try to make visible my secret visions and insights."

Similarly, chemists don't model with their molecular models what the outer eye sees. Water, for instance, is a colorless liquid, not red balls attached by sticks to smaller white balls. Rather, they try to make visible their "secret visions and insights" regarding what, through imagination, their inner eyes see.

"The hydrogen is rising. As it does so, air is coming in the bottom to take its place. So we're gradually getting a mixture of hydrogen and air in the bell jar." [Audience chatter]

Audience Anticipation. A show-and-tell advances successfully if at telling moments members of an audience begin to tell each other what is going to happen next. Here is a student's description of anticipation in lectures given by a famous Russian chemist who taught from demonstration-experiments.

"The most remarkable thing at Mendeleev's lectures was that the mind of the audience worked with his, anticipating the conclusions he might arrive at and feeling happy when he did reach those conclusions."

One of the present author's finest moments with a student was when the student said: "I always knew what you were going to say next." Two teaching strategies foster such remarks.

To Foster Audience Anticipation -

(1) Teach from demonstration-experiments that *tell a story*, in which each experiment follows logically from the preceeding experiment and leads logically to the next one; and -

(2) Teach in a way that features the fact that chemistry is an *inductive science*, based on *evidence* and *imagination*.

"I'm glad evolution of the experiment is gradual [continues Dr.Bent]. For that gives time for most of the hydrogen to get away. We've burning up most of it. There won't be very much left at the end of the experiment.

"We're still getting a mixture of air and hydrogen exiting the bell jar. This means we're getting an explosive mixture of gases coming out that little tube. But as long as the mixture rises rapidly in the little tube — just as with our cone separator — as long as it rises rapidly enough the flame can't go down because the mixture is rising too fast. But the more air we get in the bell jar, the denser the mixture becomes. That means it doesn't rise as fast.

"If you watch it now we see that finally it gets to the place where the flame may be able to go down. It usually gets a little bit unstable at just about that point and the flame begins to tremor and sometimes you can hear it. It vibrates fast enough to give a little sound. If I can hear it I'll tell you at just the right time and you can quiet down and maybe you'll be able to hear it.

> **Singing Flames.** Rapid up-and-down oscillation of the flame front, too rapid for the eye to see, creates an audible sound, as the flame front starts to strike down the little tube, cools off, rises, etc.

I can imagine at least that I see a little cone inside there now, just like the Bunsen burner. The explosive cone is just about ready to travel down the little tube. About this time I usually move away [laughter] at least as far as those of you in the front row. Chuckle chuckle [and it may be a good idea to have wrapped the bell jar with transparent tape, although it's large open end means that pressure of gas inside it cannot rise to dangerous levels].

> **Body Language.** Actions and displayed apparatus speak louder than words. Demo setups and demo execution transmit as fast as the eye can see and the ear can hear answers to such questions as:
>
>> Is there evidence of planning? Thinking ahead? A regard for safety?
>> Is everything in its place. Is the next demo being readied, by teammates?
>> Is there evidence of self-confidence? Experience? Wisdom?
>> Are the presenters having fun?
>> Are they well-informed? Friendly? Humorous? Enthusiastic?
>
> The "Prince of Demonstrators", as he was known in his day, offered this advice to lecture demonstrators:
>
>> "A demonstrator should appear easy and collected, undaunted and unconcerned, his thoughts about him and his mind free for the contemplation and description of his subject. His actions should not be hasty and violent but slow, easy, and natural;." MICHAEL FARADAY
>
> An observer described Faraday's style of lecturing at the Royal Institution in these words:
>
>> "He stood at the lecture table with alll his apparatus about him, the whole of it being in such perfect order that he could without fail lay his hand on the right thing at the right moment... His intruments were never in the way, and his manipulations never interfered with his discourse. He was completely master of the situation; he had his audience at his comand, as he had himself and all his belongings. He had nothing to fret him, and he could give his eloquence full sway. It was irresitable eloquence, which compelled attention and insisted upon sympathy. LADY HOLLAND

"Can you you hear it now? Listen. No, I thought I heard it. I guess it's not quite ready yet. [Pause] Of course, it's possible that the small flame will go out. But it never . . .

"Now watch it! BOOM!! [Laughter! Clapping!! More clapping!!!] I look forward to seeing you all Wednesday morning" [the day of a scheduled final exam].

Charles Bickford's Description of Dr. Bent's Lectures

Charles Bickford, a retired chemist and, earlier, graduate student at Harvard University at a time Dr. Bent was an instructor in Harvard's department of chemistry, was for a time Dr. Bent's colleague in the teaching of general chemistry at the University of Missouri. He recorded Dr. Bent's last lecture (transcribed on the previous pages) and wrote the following account of Dr. Bent's lectures.

"This recording comprises the last lecture given by Dr. Henry E. Bent, now professor emeritus at the University of Missouri, Columbia, to a freshman chemistry class. It is the final one given of a series of thousands of lectures during his long career. Hence this lecture must have had considerable meaning for him. Indeed, it must reflect some of his long experience in teaching young students. The topics of this lecture illustrate some of his favorite experiments. His description of the experiments during the execution of the experiments is full, unhurried, and in a manner deemed by Dr. Bent to afford his listeners an easy understanding of what is happening.

"One aspect of the experiments is simplicity. [No "black boxes", between viewers and viewed phenomena!] A second aspect is the boldness and daring of professor Bent in the selection of the experiments to be done. One set of experiments described in this lecture will serve well to illustrate these two aspects. This set of experiments concerns the explosion of mixtures of oxygen with finely divided matter generally termed dusts. First, for simplicity, he selects aluminum powder and oxygen, aluminum being well-known to his listeners. It is the coarsest of the powders he will use. Second he explodes a mixture of oxygen and lycopodium powder, an extremely fine powder from the realm of plants.

"Lastly, as he explains to his audience, what could be finer than molecules of hydrogen, if one may consider hydrogen molecules as dust. At this point a large bell jar set on a heavy iron tripod is being filled with hydrogen gas, which escapes from a small vent at the top of the bell jar, where it is ignited. All wait in awe as the flame becomes smaller and smaller [and a high-pitched note becomes lower and lower] and suddenly all see the hydrogen flame vanish and hear the violent explosion of hydrogen and oxygen, during which a small quantity of water is formed. The hushness of the audience ceases suddenly, replaced by normalcy and for some, at least, a much enhanced appreciation of the wonders of chemistry.

"Following his retirement, Dr. Bent has not ceased in an effort to find ways to show what the main laws of chemistry and physics are and how those laws apply to common events that people view daily. He is designing and constructing experimental apparatus that uses only common and cheap materials found where experiments are to be performed. It is good that this type of work is being done by a person who has had so much experience and moves forward with relentless persistence in an effort to attain his goal of affording simply ways for ordinary individuals to understand the chief laws of chemistry and physics."

Dr. Bent's Description of His Demonstration Equipment

The following remarks are being made on May 7, 1972, as an aid to anyone who might wish to repeat the experiments performed and described in the lecture on the earlier part of this tape.

[The remarks were prepared for novices in execution of demonstration-experiments; namely, his non-demo-doing young colleagues in the University of Missouri's general chemistry program.]

First, the **kindling temperature** of ether and carbon disulfide. 10 mL of each liquid is sufficient. I usually use a crystallizing dish 3-4" in diameter, and a second one to put out the flame. The rod is an ordinary rod perhaps 6 mm in diameter and 6" long with an end that has been enlarged in order to have a little more heat capacity.

For **spontaneous combustion of phosphorus** a typical solution might be a piece of yellow phosphorus from an 11/16" cylinder about 1/2" long dissolved in 15 mL of carbon disulfide. A pipette can be used to dribble this onto large filter paper perhaps 8-10" in diameter.

The **effect of gravity on candles' flames** is shown by using two 3 liter short-necked round bottom flasks. The candle might be 3/4" in diameter.

The **burning of air** is done with a glass tube about 35 mm in diameter and 30 cm long, with a side tube through which gas is admitted. And then at both top and bottom there is tube about 22 cm long drawn down to an opening about 12 mm in diameter so that the pressure can build up sufficiently to force the gas out the bottom.

For the **Bunsen burner** we used a large glass tube over a Meeker or Fisher burner in order to get the enlarged Bunsen burner. At first, however, we take an ordinary Bunsen burner and a piece of asbestos paper perhaps 3" wide and 10" long. This can be held at an angle in the flame to give a conic section of a cone or it can be held vertically, in which case you get two lines almost vertical, showing the high temperature at the edge of the flame.

The **safety match** with a pin about 1/4" from the head can be placed on top of the burner when the flame is out and then on igniting the flame the match does not ignite because it's inside the inner cone.

The large glass tube used with the Meeker burner to make the **Smithells Separator** is about 35 mm in diameter and 110 cm long. Then about the middle of this space is a tube about 23 mm in diameter and 20 cm long.

The Davy Safety Lamp we inherited. I suspect it cannot be obtained anywhere today [1972. 2014: They are available on the internet.]

In showing the inability of a flame to go through **wire gauze**, I use copper gauze.

For the **explosions** a cylinder perhaps 6" in diameter and 1 1/2' long is convenient. Aluminum powder, perhaps a teaspoon or two, is placed in the bottom and then the air displaced with oxygen. Finally a crystallizing watch glass is placed over the open end of the cylinder. It is shaken violently and instantly brought to a burner, which is already lit, in order to get the explosion. This has to be done very rapidly as the aluminum powder settles pretty promptly. The same is true with **lycopodium powder**: maybe a couple of teaspoons full followed by displacement of air with oxygen.

Finally for **hydrogen in a bell jar**, we use one 24 cm in diameter and 27 cm high. At the top of the bell jar is a rubber stopper carrying a little glass tube about 4 mm inside diameter and 10 cm long. This is the tube that is ignited, of course, when the hydrogen is in the bell jar. Great care must be exercised, of course, to be certain that the gas in the bell jar is not explosive. Too violent a stream of hydrogen when filling it would doubtless create turbulence and bring in air. Too small a stream might not fill it rapidly enough. [It would be useful to know what bubble rate of hydrogen through water is approximately optimal.]

Remembrance of Hydrogen in a Bell Jar. Once while waiting for a play to begin at Carnegie-Mellon University, I (Henry A. Bent) struck up a conversation with a fellow retiree seated next to me. He mentioned that he'd attended the University of Illinois.

"A famous chemistry department," I said, "with Roger Adams and others."
"I had chemistry with John Bailar," he said.
"I knew him. So did my father. I've used his textbook. A fine chemist and gentleman.
Nodding, he added: "I remember an experiment he did with a bell jar. He filled it with hydrogen. Lit it. BOOM! That was extraordinary."

Lectures may "go in one ear and out the other one" but never have I heard that said of an explosion.

Remembrance of Water Electrolyzed. Another time I was having lunch with a soon to retire university president, a political geographer raised in one of Newfoundland's outports where his pre-college schooling was in a one-room school house. When he mentioned that he'd had a course in chemistry, I asked him my usual question.

"What do you remember?"

"Three things," he said immediately. "Sodium in water. Magnesium burning in air. And the electrolysis of water: hydrogen here [gesturing] and oxygen there. That was amazing!"

Concluding Comments by Dr. Bent

A "Delightful Situation". "When we started taping chem 1 lectures, we had in mind that the tapes would be helpful for several types of students, including foreign students who have trouble with English, students who miss lectures, and students who may be slow learners. However, the most important role of the tapes in my opinion arises from the fact that they relieve conscientious students of the feeling of a need to take notes on everything he or she sees and hears. For the lecturer that is a delightful situation because you find that you are now talking to students *face-to-face*, looking into their eyes, rather than at the tops of their heads as they lean over their notebooks trying to get down what you've said while not seeing what you're doing.

An Unfortunate Situation. "Use of demonstrations in lectures has, however, declined precipitously. Some of chemistry's greatest lecturers in the past, like Edgar Fahs Smith at the University of Pennsylvania, Arthur B. Lamb at Harvard University, Joel Hildebrand at the University of California, Harry N. Holmes at Oberlin College, and Herman Schlundt at the University of Missouri relied heavily on lecture demonstrations. However, there are lecturers today, especially younger men and women in the field, who feel that it is too difficult or too time-consuming to spend time doing demonstrations [Excuses, excuses! Not the real reasons!].

An Attempt to Rectify the "Situation". "I have tried to design experiments so that they can be put back into boxes or cases, brought out on short notice, and usually in not more than two or three minutes be assembled and ready for an experiment. Only in a few instances have I done experiments where elaborate preparation is necessary each year. It is not necessary to have an assistant to set up most of my experiments when they have been properly designed."

An Obvious Necessity. For instruction in general chemistry to be based on demonstration-experiments, it's obviously necessary to have instructors who have been *properly educated* for that enterprise. Unfortunately, that's often not the situation, today, in the United States.

A Narrowing of the PhD Degree in Chemistry and Disappearance of Teaching General Chemistry in the "Grand Inspirational Manner" from Demonstration-Experiments. "General Chemistry," Pauling used to say, "is an introduction to the *entire science* of chemistry" Yet as chemistry has become increasing *general*, education of chemists has become increasingly *specialized*, owing to how, since WWII, graduate research in the U.S has been supported, by grants—with generous overhead to institutions—to individual faculty members, whose promotions and tenure have become tied, accordingly, to the level of their grant support that, in turn, is tied to their research that, in turn, is generally executed largely by their graduate students, who are, accordingly, kept in the lab *as much as possible* at work on their advisors' promotion-determining research. Gone in PhD programs in chemistry is a comprehensive minor. Gone are two language examinations. And gone are comprehensive examinations in a candidates' major, for admission to PhD programs, and, again, near their completion, during defense of a thesis. Produced are deeply but narrowly trained PhD's, well-prepared to pursue research in their specialties, but ill prepared to teach *general* chemistry from *demonstration-experiments*.

Another Attempt to Rectify the "Situation". Concerned that his young colleagues in the general chemistry program were not using the department's extraordinarily fine collection of demonstration equipment, housed in tall, glass-door-faced cabinets, almost as in a museum, immediately off the building's main lecture hall, Dr. Bent took color photographs of his demonstration set-ups, typed captions for them, as to how the apparatus might be used, and mounted the photographs in albums, which he gave to his colleagues. Their response? "Would you like to do the demos for my class?"

After Dr. Bent retired, his colleagues converted the space occupied by the demonstration equipment to research space and *trashed the equipment!* "It broke my heart," said my father.

We must earn over again what we have inherited from our fathers, said Goethe, or it will not be ours. This book attempts to promote that historic process for teaching chemistry from demonstration-experiments.

Bibliography

"What Do I Remember? The Role of Lecture Experiments in Teaching Chemistry," Henry A. Bent and Henry E. Bent, *J. Chem. Educ.*, **57**, 609 (1980).